PAPER BOAT

PAPER BOAT

NEW AND SELECTED POEMS

1961–2023

MARGARET ATWOOD

ALFRED A. KNOPF

NEW YORK

2024

THIS IS A BORZOI BOOK PUBLISHED
BY ALFRED A. KNOPF

www.aaknopf.com

Knopf, Borzoi Books, and the colophon are registered trademarks
of Penguin Random House LLC.

Owing to limitations of space, all acknowledgements to reprint
previously published material appear on pages 589–90.

LIBRARY OF CONGRESS CATALOGING-IN-PUBLICATION DATA
Names: Atwood, Margaret, [date] author.
Title: Paper boat : new and selected poems, 1961–2023 /
Margaret Atwood.
Other titles: Paper boat (compilation)
Description: First edition. | New York : Alfred A. Knopf, 2024.
Identifiers: LCCN 2023057292 | ISBN 9780593802649 (hardcover) |
ISBN 9780593802656 (ebook)
Subjects: LCGFT: Poetry.
Classification: LCC PR9199.3.A8 P37 2024 |
DDC 811/.54—dc23/eng/20231214
LC record available at https://lccn.loc.gov/2023057292

Jacket photograph © Ruven Afanador / CPi Syndication
Jacket design by Janet Hansen

Manufactured in the United States of America
First Edition

For my readers

For my family

For absent friends

And for Graeme, as always

CONTENTS

✧

SELECTED POEMS II

MORNING IN THE BURNED HOUSE

FROM

THE DOOR

FROM

DEARLY

UNCOLLECTED POEMS II
(1991–2023)

FROM

DOUBLE

PERSEPHONE

✧ ✧ ✧

FORMAL GARDEN

The girl with the gorgon touch
Stretches a glad hand to each
New piper peddling beds of roses
Hoping to find within her reach

At last, a living wrist and arm
Petals that will crush and fade
But always she meets a marbled flesh
A fixing eye, a stiffened form
Where leaves turn spears along the glade

Behind, a line of statues stands
All with the same white oval face
And attitude of outstretched hands
Curved in an all-too-perfect grace.

From her all springs arise
To her all falls return
The articulate flesh, the singing bone
Root flower and fern;

The dancing girl's a withered crone;
Though her deceptive smile
Lures life from earth, rain from the sky,
It hides a wicked sickle; while
Those watching sense the red blood curled
Waiting, in the centre of her eye;

But the stranger from the hill
Sees only the bright gleam
Of a slim woman gathering asphodel,
And lashes his black team.

The field of hieroglyphics lies
Open under graven skies
But kneeling in the shadowed wood
No flower of air can do her good
Where letters grown from branch and stem
Have no green leaves enclosing them
Four lovers stand around her bed
One for body   one for head
Which break in bloom as soon as words
Drop from the furrowing tongues dark swords
One to press her heart to clay
One to carry her soul away
The bright feet bleed upon the grass
Freezing motion as they pass
As gathering words as cruel as thorns
She wanders with her unicorns
While the black horses of her breath
Stamp impatient for her death
And when word thorn leaf letter blossom fall
These woods loves hooves will trample all.

UNCOLLECTED

POEMS I

✦ ✦ ✦

I practise the outworn Victorian art
Of hooking wool roses to cover
The piano legs; limbs rather; but under
These ornate surfaces, the hard
Naked wood is still there.

I am industrious and clever
With my hands: I execute in paint
Landscapes on doorpanels and screens.
Down my arranged vistas, furniture
And pillows flourish in plump scenery

And on my table stands a miniature
Lemon tree in a small china garden.
It is prudent to thus restrain one's eden
Indoors. I never eat my bitter lemons
And everything remains in its own spot

Except the devil, who is under the piano
With a fringed purple tablecloth over
Him. I hear him sucking lemon rinds.
I cannot make him blend with my decor
Even with roses: his tail sticks out behind.

The moon
Shines through her when
She walks this road, the grass
Does not bend; her hands
Melt into all they touch; her eyes
Are blind as stone.

Yet she remains
In those she has passed
Through, like ripples washed in sand
By vanished water
And her dumb voice, an echo in void
Air, becomes
A singing in the ear:

I am the fear
That forms for you at corners;
I am the reflection in the lake.
I am the dead of night; I am the light
In which you shrivel, on the dark
That racks you, and the rock
On which you break.

THE SLIDESHOW

He carries Reality around with him
In a flat box

And the Aunts and Uncles in the living
Room, sitting in the dark, stare
Intently as through a window
At the screen's bright square

Looking for themselves. They have lost
Something, they have lost their past,
And he brings Redemption and all
Certainty back at last:

There are the Aunts and Uncles
Standing waving in front of the Brock
Monument, or above Niagara Falls,
Or beside the Flower Clock,

Or level beds of red tulips
Stretching for miles and miles
Anywhere, on one of those trips,
Glossy as the Aunts' red smiles . . .

That is what it was like,
They sigh, knowing that the sun shone
Always, and the sky was deep blue, like
That. But the lights go on

And he carries Reality away with him
In a flat box.

HOUSES

Somehow
Every house I live in seems to
Take the same texture

Paper
Peels when I enter
Any room and what it once concealed
Lath and plaster
Shows like dirty underwear
Under a torn skirt

Not only that
But things get scattered
How can I
Hold walls together when the bricks
Keep falling out

I sit in the centre
Of every house I live in
And the old tattered
Husk of place expands
In every heavy wind

Somehow out and out
Of sight almost until
What was all outside
Is inside really.

THE

CIRCLE

GAME

✦ ✦ ✦

It was taken some time ago.
At first it seems to be
a smeared
print: blurred lines and grey flecks
blended with the paper;

then, as you scan
it, you see in the left-hand corner
a thing that is like a branch: part of a tree
(balsam or spruce) emerging
and, to the right, halfway up
what ought to be a gentle
slope, a small frame house.

In the background there is a lake,
and beyond that, some low hills.

(The photograph was taken
the day after I drowned.

I am in the lake, in the centre
of the picture, just under the surface.

It is difficult to say where
precisely, or to say
how large or small I am:
the effect of water
on light is a distortion

but if you look long enough,
eventually
you will be able to see me.)

We must be the only ones
left, in the mist that has risen
everywhere as well
as in these woods

I walk across the bridge
towards the safety of high ground
(the tops of the trees are like islands)

gathering the sunken
bones of the drowned mothers
(hard and round in my hands)
while the white mist washes
around my legs like water;

fish must be swimming
down in the forest beneath us,
like birds, from tree to tree
and a mile away
the city, wide and silent,
is lying lost, far undersea.

You saunter beside me, talking
of the beauty of the morning,
not even knowing
that there has been a flood,

tossing small pebbles
at random over your shoulder
into the deep thick air,

not hearing the first stumbling
footsteps of the almost-born
coming (slowly) behind us,
not seeing
the almost-human
brutal faces forming
(slowly)
out of stone.

This year in my ravines
it was warm for a long time
although the leaves fell early
and my old men, re-
membering themselves
walked waist-high through
the yellow grass
in my ravines, through
alders and purple
fireweed, with burrs
catching on their sleeves,

watching the small boys climbing
in the leafless trees
or throwing pebbles
at tin cans floating
in the valley creek, or following
the hard paths worn by former
walkers or the hooves
of riding-stable horses

and at night
they slept under the bridges
of the city in my (still)
ravines

old men, ravelled as thistles
their clothing gone to seed
their beards cut stubble

while the young boys
climbed and swung
above them wildly
in the leafless eyelid
veins and branches

of a bloodred night
falling, bursting purple
as ancient rage, in

old men's
dreams of slaughter
dreams of
(impossible)
flight.

MAN WITH A HOOK

This man I
know (about a year
ago, when he was young) blew
his arm off in the cellar
making bombs
to explode the robins
on the lawns.

Now he has a hook
instead of hand;

It is an ingenious
gadget, and comes
with various attachments:
knife for meals,
pink plastic hand for everyday
handshakes, black stuffed leather glove
for social functions.

I attempt pity

But, Look, he says, glittering
like a fanatic, My hook
is an improvement:

        and to demonstrate
lowers his arm: the steel question
mark turns and opens,
and from his burning
cigarette
        unscrews
and holds the delicate
ash: a thing
precise
my clumsy tender-
skinned pink fingers
couldn't do.

I

The children on the lawn
joined hand to hand
go round and round

each arm going into
the next arm, around
full circle
until it comes
back into each of the single
bodies again

They are singing, but
not to each other:
their feet move
almost in time to the singing

We can see
the concentration on
their faces, their eyes
fixed on the empty
moving spaces just in
front of them.

We might mistake this
tranced moving for joy
but there is no joy in it

We can see (arm in arm)
as we watch them go
round and round
intent, almost
studious (the grass
underfoot ignored, the trees

circling the lawn
ignored, the lake ignored)
that the whole point

for them
of going round and round
is (faster
        slower)
going round and round

        II

Being with you
here, in this room

is like groping through a mirror
whose glass has melted
to the consistency
of gelatin

You refuse to be
(and I)
an exact reflection, yet
will not walk from the glass,
be separate.

Anyway, it is right
that they have put
so many mirrors here
(chipped, hung crooked)
in this room with its high transom
and empty wardrobe; even
the back of the door
has one.

There are people in the next room
arguing, opening and closing drawers
(the walls are thin)

You look past me, listening
to them, perhaps, or
watching
your own reflection somewhere
behind my head,
over my shoulder

You shift, and the bed
sags under us, losing its focus

There is someone in the next room

There is always

(your face
remote, listening)

someone in the next room.

III

However,
in all their games
there seems
to be some reason

however
abstract they
at first appear

When we read them legends
in the evening
of monstrous battles, and secret
betrayals in the forest
and brutal deaths,

they scarcely listened;
one yawned and fidgeted; another
chewed the wooden handle
of a hammer;
the youngest one examined
a slight cut on his toe,

and we wondered how
they could remain
completely without fear
or even interest
as the final sword slid through
the dying hero.

The next night
walking along the beach
we found the trenches
they had been making:
fortified with pointed sticks
driven into the sides
of their sand moats

and a lake-enclosed island
with no bridges:

a last attempt
(however
eroded by the water
in an hour)
to make
maybe, a refuge human
and secure from the reach

of whatever walks along
(sword hearted)
these night beaches.

IV

Returning to the room:
I notice how
all your word-
plays, calculated ploys
of the body, the witticisms
of touch, are now
attempts to keep me
at a certain distance
and (at length) avoid
admitting I am here

I watch you
watching my face
indifferently
yet with the same taut curiosity
with which you might regard
a suddenly discovered part
of your own body:
a wart perhaps,

and I remember that
you said
in childhood you were
a tracer of maps
(not making but) moving
a pen or a forefinger
over the courses of the rivers,
the different colours
that mark the rise of mountains;
a memorizer
of names (to hold
these places
in their proper places)

So now you trace me
like a country's boundary

or a strange new wrinkle in
your own well-known skin

and I am fixed, stuck
down on the outspread map
of this room, of your mind's continent
        (here and yet not here, like
        the wardrobe and the mirrors
        the voices through the wall
        your body ignored on the bed),

transfixed
by your eyes'
cold blue thumbtacks

        V

The children like the block
of grey stone that was once a fort
but now is a museum:

especially
they like the guns
and the armour brought from
other times and countries

and when they go home
their drawings will be full
for some days of swords
archaic sunburst maces
broken spears
and vivid red explosions.

While they explore
the cannons
(they aren't our children)

we walk outside along
the earthworks, noting
how they are crumbling
under the unceasing
attacks of feet and flower roots;

The weapons
that were once outside
sharpening themselves on war
are now indoors
there, in the fortress,
fragile
in glass cases;

Why is it
(I'm thinking
of the careful moulding
round the stonework archways)
that in this time, such
elaborate defences keep
things that are no longer
(much)
worth defending?

    VI

And you play the safe game
the orphan game

the ragged winter game
that says, I am alone

(hungry: I know you want me
to play it also)

the game of the waif who stands
at every picture window,

shivering, pinched nose pressed
against the glass, the snow
collecting on his neck,
watching the happy families

(a game of envy)

Yet he despises them: they are so
Victorian Christmas card:
the cheap paper shows
under the pigments of
their cheerful fire-
places and satin-
ribboned suburban laughter
and they have their own forms
of parlour
games: father and mother
playing father and mother

He's glad
to be left
out by himself
in the cold

(hugging himself).

When I tell you this,
you say (with a smile fake
as a tinsel icicle):

You do it too.

Which in some ways
is a lic, but also I suppose
is right, as usual:

although I tend to pose
in other seasons
outside other windows.

VII

Summer again;
in the mirrors of this room
the children wheel, singing
the same song;

This casual bed
scruffy as dry turf,
the counterpane
rumpled with small burrows, is
their grassy lawn

and these scuffed walls
contain their circling trees,
that low clogged sink
their lake

(a wasp comes,
drawn by the piece of sandwich
left on the nearby beach
        (how carefully you do
        such details);
one of the children flinches
but won't let go)

You make them
turn and turn, according to
the closed rules of your games,
but there is no joy in it

and as we lie
arm in arm, neither
joined nor separate
        (your observations change me
        to a spineless woman in
        a cage of bones, obsolete fort
        pulled inside out),

our lips moving
almost in time to their singing,

listening to the opening
and closing of the drawers
in the next room

(of course there is always
danger but where
would you locate it)

(the children spin
a round cage of glass
from the warm air
with their thread-thin
insect voices)

and as we lie
here, caught
in the monotony of wandering
from room to room, shifting
the place of our defences,

I want to break
these bones, your prisoning rhythms
        (winter,
        summer)
all the glass cases,

erase all maps,
crack the protecting
eggshell of your turning
singing children:

I want the circle
broken.

I) TOTEMS

We went to the park
where they kept the wooden people:
static, multiple
uprooted and trans-
planted.

Their faces were restored,
Freshly painted.
In front of them
the other wooden people
posed for each other's cameras
and nearby a new booth
sold replicas and souvenirs.

One of the people was real.
It lay on its back, smashed
by a toppling fall or just
the enduring of minor winters.
Only one of the heads had
survived intact, and it was
also beginning to decay
but there was a
life in the progressing
of old wood back to
the earth, obliteration

that the clear-hewn
standing figures lacked.

As for us, perennial watchers,
tourists of another kind
there is nothing for us to worship;

no pictures of ourselves, no blue-
sky summer fetishes, no postcards
we can either buy, or
smiling
be.

There are few totems that remain
living for us.
Though in passing,
through glass we notice

dead trees in the seared meadows
dead roots bleaching in the swamps.

II) PEBBLES

Talking was difficult. Instead
we gathered coloured pebbles
from the places on the beach
where they occurred.

They were sea-smoothed, sea-completed.
They enclosed what they intended
to mean in shapes
as random and necessary
as the shapes of words

and when finally
we spoke
the sounds of our voices fell
into the air   single and
solid and rounded and really
there
and then dulled, and then like sounds
gone,   a fistful of gathered
pebbles there was no point
in taking home, dropped on a beachful
of other coloured pebbles

and when we turned to go
a flock of small
birds flew scattered by the
fright of our sudden moving
and disappeared: hard

sea pebbles
thrown solid for an instant
against the sky

flight of words

III) CARVED ANIMALS

The small carved
animal is passed from
hand to hand
around the circle
until the stone grows warm

touching, the hands do not know
the form of animal
which was made or
the true form of stone
uncovered

and the hands, the fingers the
hidden small bones
of the hands bend to hold the shape,
shape themselves, grow
cold with the stone's cold, grow
also animal, exchange
until the skin wonders
if stone is human

In the darkness later
and even when the animal
has gone, they keep

the image of that
inner shape

hands holding warm
hands holding
the half-formed air

A second after
the first boat touched the shore,
there was a quick skirmish
brief as a twinge
and then the land was settled

(of course there was really
no shore: the water turned
to land by having
objects in it: caught and kept
from surge, made
less than immense
by networks of
roads and grids of fences)

and as for us, who drifted
picked by the sharks
during so many bluegreen
centuries before they came:
they found us
inland, stranded
on a ridge of bedrock,
defining our own island.

From our inarticulate
skeleton (so
intermixed, one
carcass),
they postulated wolves.

They dug us down
into the solid granite
where our bones grew flesh again,
came up trees and
grass.

Still
we are the salt
seas that uphold these lands.

Now horses graze
inside this fence of ribs, and

children run, with green
smiles, (not knowing
where) across
the fields of our open hands.

FROM

THE ANIMALS
IN THAT
COUNTRY

✧ ✧ ✧

THE ANIMALS IN THAT COUNTRY

In that country the animals
have the faces of people:

the ceremonial
cats possessing the streets

the fox run
politely to earth, the huntsmen
standing around him, fixed
in their tapestry of manners

the bull, embroidered
with blood and given
an elegant death, trumpets, his name
stamped on him, heraldic brand
because

(when he rolled
on the sand, sword in his heart, the teeth
in his blue mouth were human)

he is really a man

even the wolves, holding resonant
conversations in their
forests thickened with legend.

> In this country the animals
> have the faces of
> animals.
>
> Their eyes
> flash once in car headlights
> and are gone.

Their deaths are not elegant.

They have the faces of
no one.

By the felled trees, their stems
snipped neatly as though by scissors
we could tell where they had been,
the surveyors,
        clearing
their trail of single reason
(with a chainsaw it was easy
as ruling a line with a pencil)
through a land where geometries are multiple.

We followed the cut stumps,
their thumbprints, measurements
blazed in red paint: numbers and brash
letters, incongruous against
sheared wood or glacial rock

and we saw too how these vivid
signals, painted assertions

were as we looked surrounded, changed
by the gradual pressures of endless
green on the eyes, the diffused
weight of summer, the many branches

to signs without motion, red arrows
pointing in no direction; faint ritual
markings leached by time
of any meaning:

red vestiges of an erased
people, a broken
line

THE GREEN MAN

For the Boston Strangler

The green man, before whom
the doors melted,

the window man, the furnace man, the electric
light man,
the necessary man, always expected.

He said the right words,
they opened the doors;

He turned towards them
his face, a clear mirror
because he had no features.

In it they saw reflected their
own sanity;

They saw him as a function.

They did not look
in his green pockets, where he kept

    his hands changing their shape

    his hands held for them
    the necessary always
    expected emptiness

his no identification
card, his no
person

The green man,
turning their heads quietly
towards the doors, behind whom
the doors closed.

This is the lair of the landlady.

She is
a raw voice
loose in the rooms beneath me,

the continuous henyard
squabble going on below
thought in this house like
the bicker of blood through the head.

She is everywhere, intrusive as the smells
that bulge in under my doorsill;
she presides over my
meagre eating, generates
the light for eyestrain.

From her I rent my time:
she slams
my days like doors.
Nothing is mine

and when I dream images
of daring escapes through the snow
I find myself walking
always over a vast face
which is the land-
lady's, and wake up shouting.

She is a bulk, a knot
swollen in space. Though I have tried
to find some way around
her, my senses
are cluttered by perception
and can't see through her.

She stands there, a raucous fact
blocking my way:
immutable, a slab
of what is real,

solid as bacon.

There is my country under glass,
a white relief-
map with red dots for the cities,
reduced to the size of a wall

and beside it 10 blown-up snapshots
one for each province,
in purple-browns and odd reds,
the green of the trees dulled;
all blues however
of an assertive purity.

Mountains and lakes and more lakes
(though Quebec is a restaurant and Ontario the empty
interior of the parliament buildings),
with nobody climbing the trails and hauling out
the fish and splashing in the water

but arrangements of grinning tourists—
look here, Saskatchewan
is a flat lake, some convenient rocks
where two children pose with a father
and the mother is cooking something
in immaculate slacks by a smokeless fire,
her teeth white as detergent.

Whose dream is this, I would like to know:
is this a manufactured
hallucination, a cynical fiction, a lure
for export only?

I seem to remember people,
at least in the cities, also slush,
machines and assorted garbage. Perhaps
that was my private mirage

which will just evaporate
when I go back. Or the citizens will be gone,
run off to the peculiarly
green forests
to wait among the brownish mountains
for the platoons of tourists
and plan their odd red massacres.

Unsuspecting
window lady, I ask you:

Do you see nothing
watching you from under the water?

Was the sky ever that blue?

Who really lives there?

Who locked me

into this crazed man-made
stone brain
        where the weathered
totempole jabs a blunt
finger at the byzantine
mosaic dome

Under that ornate
golden cranium I wander
among fragments of gods, tarnished
coins, embalmed gestures
chronologically arranged,
looking for the EXIT sign

but in spite of the diagrams
at every corner, labelled
in red: YOU ARE HERE
the labyrinth holds me,

turning me around
the cafeteria, the washrooms,
a spiral through marble
Greece and Rome, the bronze
horses of China

then past the carved masks, wood and fur
to where 5 plaster Indians
in a glass case
squat near a dusty fire

and further, confronting me
with a skeleton child, preserved
in the desert air, curled
beside a clay pot and a few beads.

I say I am far
enough,   stop here   please
no more

but the perverse museum, corridor
by corridor, an idiot
voice jogged by a pushed
button, repeats its memories

and I am dragged to the mind's
deadend, the roar of the bone-
yard, I am lost
among the mastodons
and beyond: a fossil
shell, then

samples of rocks
and minerals, even the thundering
tusks dwindling to pin-
points in the stellar
fluorescent-lighted
wastes of geology

ELEGY FOR THE GIANT TORTOISES

Let others pray for the passenger pigeon
the dodo, the whooping crane, the eskimo:
everyone must specialize

I will confine myself to a meditation
upon the giant tortoises
withering finally on a remote island.

I concentrate in subway stations,
in parks, I can't quite see them,
they move to the peripheries of my eyes

but on the last day they will be there;
already the event
like a wave travelling shapes vision:

on the road where I stand they will materialize,
plodding past me in a straggling line
awkward without water

their small heads pondering
from side to side, their useless armour
sadder than tanks and history,

in their closed gaze ocean and sunlight paralyzed,
lumbering up the steps, under the archways
towards the square glass altars

where the brittle gods are kept,
the relics of what we have destroyed,
our holy and obsolete symbols.

ROOMINGHOUSE, WINTER

Catprints, dogprints, marks
of ancient children
have made the paths we follow

to the vestibule, piled
with overshoes, ownerless letters
a wooden sled.

The threadbare treads
on the stairs. The trails
worn by alien feet

in time through the forest snowdrifts
of the corridor to this remnant, this
discarded door

What disturbs me in the bathroom
is the unclaimed toothbrush.

In the room itself, none
of the furniture is mine.

The plates are on the table
to weight it down.

I call you sometimes
to make sure you are still there.

Tomorrow, when you come to dinner
they will tell you I never lived here.

My window is a funnel
for the shapes of chaos

In the backyard, frozen bones, the children's
voices, derelict
objects

Inside, the wall
buckles; the pressure

balanced by this clear
small silence.

We must resist. We must refuse
to disappear

I said, In exile
survival
is the first necessity.

After that (I say this
tentatively)
we might begin

Survive what? you said.

In the weak light you looked
over your shoulder.
                    You said

Nobody ever survives.

SPEECHES FOR DR. FRANKENSTEIN

I

I, the performer
in the tense arena, glittered
under the fluorescent moon. Was bent
masked by the table. Saw what focused
my intent: the emptiness

The air filled with an ether of cheers.

My wrist extended a scalpel.

II

The table is a flat void,
barren as total freedom. Though behold

A sharp twist
like taking a jar top off

and it is a living
skeleton, mine, round,
that lies on the plate before me

red as a pomegranate,
every cell a hot light.

III

I circle, confront
my opponent. The thing

refuses to be shaped, it moves
like yeast. I thrust,

the thing fights back.
It dissolves, growls, grows crude claws;

The air is dusty with blood.

It springs. I cut
with delicate precision.

The specimens
ranged on the shelves, applaud.

The thing falls Thud. A cat
anatomized.

O secret
form of the heart, now I have you.

IV

Now I shall ornament you.
What would you like?

Baroque scrolls on your ankles?
A silver navel?

I am the universal weaver;
I have eight fingers.

I complicate you;
I surround you with intricate ropes.

What web shall I wrap you in?
Gradually I pin you down.

What equation shall
I carve and seal in your skull?

What size will I make you?
Where should I put your eyes?

V

I was insane with skill:
I made you perfect.

I should have chosen instead
to curl you small as a seed,

trusted beginnings. Now I wince
before this plateful of results:

core and rind, the flesh between
already turning rotten.

I stand in the presence
of the destroyed god:

a rubble of tendons,
knuckles and raw sinews.

Knowing that the work is mine
how can I love you?

These archives of potential
time exude fear like a smell.

VI

You arise, larval
and shrouded in the flesh I gave you;

I, who have no covering
left but a white cloth skin

escape from you. You are red,
you are human and distorted.

You have been starved,
you are hungry. I have nothing to feed you.

I pull around me, running,
a cape of rain.

What was my ravenous motive?
Why did I make you?

VII

Reflection, you have stolen
everything you needed:

my joy, my ability
to suffer.

You have transmuted
yourself to me: I am
a vestige, I am numb.

Now you accuse me of murder.

Can't you see
I am incapable?

Blood of my brain,
it is you who have killed these people.

VIII

Since I dared
to attempt impious wonders

I must pursue
that animal I once denied
was mine.

Over this vacant winter
plain, the sky is a black shell;
I move within it, a cold
kernel of pain.

I scratch huge rescue messages
on the solid
snow; in vain. My heart's
husk is a stomach. I am its food.

IX

The sparkling monster
gambols there ahead,
his mane electric:
This is his true place.

He dances in spirals on the ice,
his clawed feet
kindling shaggy fires.

His happiness
is now the chase itself:
he traces it in light,
his paths contain it.

I am the gaunt hunter
necessary for his patterns,
lurking, gnawing leather.

X

The creature, his arctic hackles
bristling, spreads
over the dark ceiling,
his paws on the horizons,
rolling the world like a snowball.

He glows and says:

Doctor, my shadow
shivering on the table,
you dangle on the leash
of your own longing;
your need grows teeth.

You sliced me loose

and said it was
Creation. I could feel the knife.
Now you would like to heal
that chasm in your side,
but I recede. I prowl.

I will not come when you call.

THE REINCARNATION OF CAPTAIN COOK

Earlier than I could learn
the maps had been coloured in.
When I pleaded, the kings told me
nothing was left to explore.

I set out anyway, but
everywhere I went
there were historians, wearing
wreaths and fake teeth
belts; or in the deserts, cairns
and tourists. Even the caves had
candle stubs, inscriptions quickly
scribbled in darkness. I could

never arrive. Always
the names got there before.

Now I am old I know my
mistake was my acknowledging
of maps. The eyes raise
tired monuments.

Burn down
the atlases, I shout
to the park benches; and go

past the cenotaph
waving a blank banner
across the street, beyond
the corner

into a new land cleaned of geographies,
its beach gleaming with arrows.

FROM

THE

JOURNALS

OF

SUSANNA

MOODIE

✦ ✦ ✦

JOURNAL I

(1832–1840)

✧

ls it my clothes, my way of walking,
the things I carry in my hand
—a book, a bag with knitting—
the incongruous pink of my shawl

this space cannot hear

or is it my own lack
of conviction which makes
these vistas of desolation,
long hills, the swamps, the barren sand, the glare
of sun on the bone-white
driftlogs, omens of winter,
the moon alien in day-
time a thin refusal

The others leap, shout

       Freedom!

The moving water will not show me
my reflection.

The rocks ignore.

I am a word
in a foreign language.

After we had crossed the long illness
that was the ocean, we sailed upriver

On the first island
the immigrants threw off their clothes
and danced like sandflies

We left behind one by one
the cities rotting with cholera,
one by one our civilized
distinctions

and entered a large darkness.

It was our own
ignorance we entered.

I have not come out yet

My brain gropes nervous
tentacles in the night, sends out
fears hairy as bears,
demands lamps; or waiting

for my shadowy husband, hears
malice in the trees' whispers.

I need wolf's eyes to see
the truth.

I refuse to look in a mirror.

Whether the wilderness is
real or not
depends on who lives there.

They move between the jagged edge
of the forest and the jagged river
on a stumpy patch of cleared land

my husband, a neighbour, another man
weeding the few rows
of string beans and dusty potatoes.

They bend, straighten; the sun
lights up their faces and hands, candles
flickering in the wind against the

unbright earth. I see them; I know
none of them believe they are here.
They deny the ground they stand on,

pretend this dirt is the future.
And they are right. If they let go
of that illusion solid to them as a shovel,

open their eyes even for a moment
to these trees, to this particular sun
they would be surrounded, stormed, broken

in upon by branches, roots, tendrils, the dark
side of light
as I am.

One, the summer fire
outside: the trees melting, returning
to their first red elements
on all sides, cutting me off
from escape or the saving
lake

I sat in the house, raised up
between that shapeless raging
and my sleeping children
a charm: concentrate on
form, geometry, the human
architecture of the house, square
closed doors, proved roofbeams,
the logic of windows

(the children could not be wakened:
in their calm dreaming
the trees were straight and still
had branches and were green)

The other, the winter
fire inside: the protective roof
shrivelling overhead, the rafters
incandescent, all those corners
and straight lines flaming, the carefully
made structure
prisoning us in a cage of blazing
bars
      the children
were awake and crying;
I wrapped them, carried them
outside into the snow.
Then I tried to rescue
what was left of their scorched dream

about the house: blankets,
warm clothes, the singed furniture
of safety cast away with them
in a white chaos

Two fires in-
formed me,

(each refuge fails
us; each danger
becomes a haven)

left charred marks
now around which I
try to grow

It was as if I woke
after a sleep of seven years

to find stiff lace, religious
black rotted
off by earth and the strong waters

and instead my skin thickened
with bark and the white hairs of roots

My heirloom face I brought
with me a crushed eggshell
among other debris:
the china plate shattered
on the forest road, the shawl
from India decayed, pieces of letters

and the sun here had stained
me its barbarous colour

Hands grown stiff, the fingers
brittle as twigs
eyes bewildered after
seven years, and almost
blind / buds, which can see
only the wind

the mouth cracking
open like a rock in fire
trying to say

What is this

(you find only
the shape you already are
but what
if you have forgotten that
or discover you
have never known)

I, who had been erased
by fire, was crept in
upon by green
                    (how
lucid a season)
                In time the animals
arrived to inhabit me,

first one
  by one, stealthily
(their habitual traces
burnt); then
having marked new boundaries
returning, more
confident, year
by year, two
by two

but restless: I was not ready
altogether to be moved into

They could tell I was
too heavy: I might
capsize;

I was frightened
by their eyes (green or
amber) glowing out from inside me

I was not completed; at night
I could not see without lanterns.

He wrote, We are leaving. I said
I have no clothes
left I can wear

The snow came. The sleigh was a relief;
its track lengthened behind,
pushing me towards the city

and rounding the first hill, I was
(instantaneous)
unlived in: they had gone.

There was something they almost taught me
I came away not having learned.

JOURNAL II

(1840–1871)

✧

DEATH OF A YOUNG SON BY DROWNING

He, who navigated with success
the dangerous river of his own birth
once more set forth

on a voyage of discovery
into the land I floated on
but could not touch to claim.

His feet slid on the bank,
the currents took him;
he swirled with ice and trees in the swollen water

and plunged into distant regions,
his head a bathysphere;
through his eyes' thin glass bubbles

he looked out, reckless adventurer
on a landscape stranger than Uranus
we have all been to and some remember.

There was an accident; the air locked,
he was hung in the river like a heart.
They retrieved the swamped body,

cairn of my plans and future charts,
with poles and hooks
from among the nudging logs.

It was spring, the sun kept shining, the new grass
leapt to solidity;
my hands glistened with details.

After the long trip I was tired of waves.
My foot hit rock. The dreamed sails
collapsed, ragged.

        I planted him in this country
        like a flag.

THE IMMIGRANTS

They are allowed to inherit
the sidewalks involved as palmlines, bricks
exhausted and soft, the deep
lawnsmells, orchards whorled
to the land's contours, the inflected weather

only to be told they are too poor
to keep it up, or someone
has noticed and wants to kill them; or the towns
pass laws which declare them obsolete.

I see them coming
up from the hold smelling of vomit,
infested, emaciated, their skins grey
with travel; as they step on shore

the old countries recede, become
perfect, thumbnail castles preserved
like gallstones in a glass bottle, the
towns dwindle upon the hillsides
in a light paperweight-clear.

They carry their carpetbags and trunks
with clothes, dishes, the family pictures;
they think they will make an order
like the old one, sow miniature orchards,
carve children and flocks out of wood

but always they are too poor, the sky
is flat, the green fruit shrivels
in the prairie sun, wood is for burning;
and if they go back, the towns

in time have crumbled, their tongues
stumble among awkward teeth, their ears

are filled with the sound of breaking glass.
I wish I could forget them
and so forget myself:

my mind is a wide pink map
across which move year after year
arrows and dotted lines, further and further,
people in railway cars

their heads stuck out of the windows
at stations, drinking milk or singing,
their features hidden with beards or shawls
day and night riding across an ocean of unknown
land to an unknown land.

DREAM 1: THE BUSH GARDEN

I stood once more in that garden
sold, deserted and
gone to seed

In the dream I could
see down through the earth, could see
the potatoes curled
like pale grubs in the soil
the radishes thrusting down
their fleshy snouts, the beets
pulsing like slow amphibian hearts

Around my feet
the strawberries were surging, huge
and shining

When I bent
to pick, my hands
came away red and wet

In the dream I said
I should have known
anything planted here
would come up blood

"They capped their heads with feathers, masked
their faces, wore their clothes backwards, howled
with torches through the midnight winter

and dragged the black man from his house
to the jolting music of broken
instruments, pretending to each other

it was a joke, until
they killed him. I don't know
what happened to the white bride."

The American lady, adding she
thought it was a disgraceful piece
of business, finished her tea.

(Note: Never pretend this isn't
part of the soil too, teadrinkers, and inadvertent
victims and murderers, when we come this way

again in other forms, take care
to look behind, within
where the skeleton face beneath

the face puts on its feather mask, the arm
within the arm lifts up the spear:
Resist those cracked

drumbeats. Stop this. Become human.)

THE DOUBLE VOICE

Two voices
took turns using my eyes:

One had manners,
painted in watercolours,
used hushed tones when speaking
of mountains or Niagara Falls,
composed uplifting verse
and expended sentiment upon the poor.

The other voice
had other knowledge:
that men sweat
always and drink often,
that pigs are pigs
but must be eaten
anyway, that unborn babies
fester like wounds in the body,
that there is nothing to be done
about mosquitoes;

One saw through my
bleared and gradually
bleaching eyes, red leaves,
the rituals of seasons and rivers

The other found a dead dog
jubilant with maggots
half-buried among the sweet peas.

JOURNAL III

(1871–1969)

✧

DAGUERREOTYPE TAKEN IN OLD AGE

I know I change
have changed

but whose is this vapid face
pitted and vast, rotund
suspended in empty paper
as though in a telescope

the granular moon

I rise from my chair
pulling against gravity
I turn away
and go out into the garden

I revolve among the vegetables,
my head ponderous
reflecting the sun
in shadows from the pocked ravines
cut in my cheeks, my eye-
sockets 2 craters

along the paths
I orbit
the apple trees
white white spinning
stars around me

I am being
eaten away by light

The streets are new, the harbour
is new also;
the lunatic asylum is yellow.

On the first floor there were
women sitting, sewing;
they looked at us sadly, gently,
answered questions.

On the second floor there were
women crouching, thrashing,
tearing off their clothes, screaming;
to us they paid little attention.

On the third floor
I went through a glass-panelled
door into a different kind of room.
It was a hill, with boulders, trees, no houses.
I sat down and smoothed my gloves.

The landscape was saying something
but I couldn't hear. One of the rocks
sighed and rolled over.

Above me, at eye level
three faces appeared in an oblong space.

They wanted me to go out
to where there were streets and
the Toronto harbour

I shook my head. There were no clouds, the flowers
deep red and feathered, shot from among
the dry stones,
         the air
was about to tell me
all kinds of answers

RESURRECTION

I see now I see
now I cannot see

earth is a blizzard in my eyes

I hear now

       the rustle of the snow

the angels listening above me

       thistles bright with sleet
       gathering

waiting for the time
to reach me
up to the pillared
sun, the final city

       or living towers

unrisen yet
whose dormant stones lie folding
their holy fire around me

       (but the land shifts with frost
       and those who have become the stone
       voices of the land
       shift also and say

       god is not
       the voice in the whirlwind

       god is the whirlwind

       at the last
       judgment we will all be trees

A BUS ALONG ST. CLAIR: DECEMBER

It would take more than that to banish
me: this is my kingdom still.

Turn, look up
through the gritty window: an unexplored
wilderness of wires

Though they buried me in monuments
of concrete slabs, of cables
though they mounded a pyramid
of cold light over my head
though they said, We will build
silver paradise with a bulldozer

it shows how little they know
about vanishing: I have
my ways of getting through.

Right now, the snow
is no more familiar
to you than it was to me:
this is my doing.
The grey air, the roar
going on behind it
are no more familiar.

I am the old woman
sitting across from you on the bus,
her shoulders drawn up like a shawl;
out of her eyes come secret
hatpins, destroying
the walls, the ceiling

Turn, look down:
there is no city;
this is the centre of a forest

your place is empty

FROM

PROCEDURES

FOR

UNDERGROUND

✧ ✧ ✧

EDEN IS A ZOO

I keep my parents in a garden
among lumpy trees, green sponges
on popsicle sticks. I give them a lopsided
sun which drops its heat
in spokes the colour of yellow crayon.

They have thick elephant legs,
quills for hair and tiny heads;
they clump about under the trees
dressed in the clothes of thirty years
ago, on them innocent as plain skin.

Are they bewildered when they come across
corners of rooms in the forest,
a tin cup shining like pearl,
a frayed pink blanket, a rusted shovel?

Does it bother them to perform
the same actions over and over,
hands gathering white flowers
by the lake or tracing designs in the sand,
a word repeated till it hangs carved
forever in the blue air?

Are they content?

Do they want to get out?

Do they see me looking at them
from across the hedge of spikes
and cardboard fire painted red
I built with so much time
and pain, but
they don't know is there?

GIRL AND HORSE, 1928

You are younger than I am, you are
someone I never knew, you stand
under a tree, your face half-shadowed,
holding the horse by its bridle.

Why do you smile?   Can't you
see the apple blossoms falling around
you, snow, sun, snow, listen, the tree
dries and is being burnt, the wind

is bending your body, your face
ripples like water   where did you go
But no, you stand there exactly
the same, you can't hear me, forty

years ago you were caught by light
and fixed in that secret
place where we live, where we believe
nothing can change, grow older.

> (On the other side
> of the picture, the instant
> is over, the shadow
> of the tree has moved. You wave,
>
> then turn and ride
> out of sight through the vanished
> orchard, still smiling
> as though you do not notice)

THE SMALL CABIN

The house we built gradually
from the ground up when we were young
(three rooms, the walls
raw trees) burned down
last year   they said

I didn't see it, and so
the house is still there in me

        among branches as always I stand
inside it looking out
at the rain moving across the lake

but when I go back
to the empty place in the forest
the house will blaze and crumple
suddenly in my mind

collapsing like a cardboard carton
thrown on a bonfire, summers
crackling, my earlier
selves outlined in flame.

Left in my head will be
the blackened earth: the truth.

Where did the house go?

Where do the words go
when we have said them?

What stands in this garden
is there because I measured, placed, reached
down into the soil and pulled out
stems, leaves, gradually:
                          fabric-
textured zinnias; asters
the colours of chintz; thick
pot-shaped marigolds, the
sunflowers brilliant as
imitations

but outside the string borders

other things raise
themselves, brief
motions at the path's edge

                    the bonewhite

plants that grow
without sunlight, flickering
in the evening forest

certain ferns; fungi
like buried feet
                  the blue
flags, ice flames
reflected in the bay
that melt when the
sun hits noon

these have their roots
in another land

they are mist

if you touch them, your
eyes go through them.

INTERVIEW WITH A TOURIST

You speed by with your camera and your spear
and stop and ask me for directions

I answer there are none

You ask me why the light here
is always the same colour;
I talk about the diffuse
surfaces, angles of refraction

You want to know why there are
no pleasant views, no distances,
why everything crowds close to the skin

I mention the heavier density
here, the thickness, the obsolescence of vistas

You ask me why the men are starved and silver
and have goggle eyes
and why the women are cold tentacled flowers

I reply with a speech about Nature

You ask me why I can't love you

It is because you have air in your lungs
and I am an average citizen

Once, when there was history
some obliterating fact occurred,
no solution was found

Now this country is underwater;
we can love only the drowned

PROCEDURES FOR UNDERGROUND

Northwest Coast

The country beneath
the earth has a green sun
and the rivers flow backwards;

the trees and rocks are the same
as they are here, but shifted.
Those who live there are always hungry;

from them you can learn
wisdom and great power,
if you can descend and return safely.

You must look for tunnels, animal
burrows or the cave in the sea
guarded by the stone man;

when you are down you will find
those who were once your friends
but they will be changed and dangerous.

Resist them, be careful
never to eat their food.
Afterwards, if you live, you will be able

to see them when they prowl as winds,
as thin sounds in our village. You will
tell us their names, what they want, who

has made them angry by forgetting them.
For this gift, as for all gifts, you must
suffer: those from the underland

will be always with you, whispering their
complaints, beckoning you
back down; while among us here

you will walk wrapped in an invisible
cloak. Few will seek your help
with love, none without fear.

Mostly the animals dream
of other animals   each
according to its kind

       (though certain mice and small rodents
       have nightmares of a huge pink
       shape with five claws descending)

: moles dream of darkness and delicate
mole smells

frogs dream of green and golden
frogs
sparkling like wet suns
among the lilies

red and black
striped fish, their eyes open
have red and black striped
dreams   defence, attack, meaningful
patterns

birds dream of territories
enclosed by singing.

Sometimes the animals dream of evil
in the form of soap and metal
but mostly the animals dream
of other animals.

There are exceptions:

       the silver fox in the roadside zoo
       dreams of digging out
       and of baby foxes, their necks bitten

the caged armadillo
near the train
station, which runs
all day in figure eights
its piglet feet pattering,
no longer dreams
but is insane when waking;

the iguana
in the petshop window on St. Catherine Street
crested, royal-eyed, ruling
its kingdom of water-dish and sawdust

dreams of sawdust.

•

A SOUL, GEOLOGICALLY

The longer we stay here the harder
it is for me to see you.

Your outline, skin
that marks you off
melts in this light

and from behind your face
the unknown areas appear:

hills yellow-pelted, dried earth
bubbles, or thrust up
steeply as knees

the sky a flat blue desert,

these spaces you fill
with their own emptiness.

Your shape wavers, glares
like heat above the road,

then you merge and extend:
you have gone,
in front of me there is a stone ridge.

Which of these forms
have you taken:

hill, tree clawed
to the rock, fallen rocks worn
and rounded by the wind

You are the wind,
you contain me

I walk in the white silences
of your mind, remembering

the way it is millions of years before
on the wide floor of the sea

while my eyes lift like continents
to the sun and erode slowly.

HABITATION

Marriage is not
a house or even a tent

it is before that, and colder:

the edge of the forest, the edge
of the desert
                    the unpainted stairs
at the back where we squat
outside, eating popcorn

the edge of the receding glacier

where painfully and with wonder
at having survived even
this far

we are learning to make fire

A lake sunken among
cedar and black spruce hills;
late afternoon.

On the ice a woman skating,
jacket sudden
red against the white,

concentrating on moving
in perfect circles.

(actually she is my mother, she is
over at the outdoor skating rink
near the cemetery. On three sides
of her there are streets of brown
brick houses; cars go by; on the
fourth side is the park building.
The snow banked around the rink
is grey with soot. She never skates
here. She's wearing a sweater and
faded maroon earmuffs, she has
taken off her gloves)

Now near the horizon
the enlarged pink sun swings down.
Soon it will be zero.

With arms wide the skater
turns, leaving her breath like a diver's
trail of bubbles.

Seeing the ice
as what it is, water:
seeing the months
as they are, the years

in sequence occurring
underfoot, watching
the miniature human
figure balanced on steel
needles (those compasses
floated in saucers) on time
sustained, above
time circling: miracle

Over all I place
a glass bell

In the daytime I am brave,
I draw my gloves on finger
by finger, my money
behaves itself in my purse
the food rolls over on my plate
there are no omens

I have everything under control

But at night the constellations
emerge; I clench
my feet to boots
my face to a wire mask

Their whitehard eyes bristle
behind the bars, their teeth
grow larger for being starved

They were once dust and ordinary
hatreds. I breathed on them, named them:
now they are predictions.

This is the way it begins:
the countryside almost flat, stretching away
from the four-lane highway, everything
green except for certain
trees which have hardened and stand
grey and fixed in the shapes life gave them,
fossil veins, dead lungs.

The cars are lined up, edging slowly
on the north lanes, the windshields
glitter, it is the city moving,
the drivers intent on getting out, getting
away from something
they carry always with them;
a hand comes out of a window
and throws away an apple core.

The sun shines down

on two cars which have collided
at a turn-off, and rest
quietly on their sides

and on some cows which have come over,
nudge each other aside
at the fence, and stare;
the people in the passing
cars stare too;

out of the blue sky and the white clouds
something is falling   falling
gently on them like invisible rain, or a blessing.

The marsh flat where they graze
beside the stream is
late afternoon, serene
with slanted light: green leaves are
yellow: even
the mud shines

Placid, they bend down
silently to the grass;
when they move, the small birds
follow, settle almost
under their feet.

Fenced out but anxious
anyway, and glad our car is
near, we press
close to the wire
squares, our hands raised
for shields
against the sun, which is
everywhere

       It was hard to see them
but we thought we saw
in the field near them, the god
of this place: brutal,
zeus-faced, his horned
head man-bearded, his
fused red eye turned inward
to cloudburst and pounded earth, the water-
falling of hooves fisted inside
a calm we would call madness.

Then they were going
in profile, one by one, their
firelit outlines fixed as carvings

backs to us now
they enter
the shade of the gold-edged trees

POWER
POLITICS

✦ ✦ ✦

✧

you fit into me
like a hook into an eye

a fish hook
an open eye

You rose from a snowbank
with three heads, all
your hands were in your pockets

I said, Haven't
I seen you somewhere before

You pretended you were hungry
I offered you sandwiches and ginger ale
but you refused

Your six eyes glowed
red, you shivered cunningly

Can't we
be friends I said;
you didn't answer.

✧

You take my hand and
I'm suddenly in a bad movie,
it goes on and on and
why am I fascinated

We waltz in slow motion
through an air stale with aphorisms
we meet behind endless potted palms
you climb through the wrong windows

Other people are leaving
but I always stay till the end
I paid my money, I
want to see what happens.

In chance bathtubs I have to
peel you off me
in the form of smoke and melted
celluloid

       Have to face it I'm
finally an addict,
the smell of popcorn and worn plush
lingers for weeks

I can change my-
self more easily
than I can change you

I could grow bark and
become a shrub

or switch back in time
to the woman image left
in cave rubble, the drowned
stomach bulbed with fertility,
face a tiny bead, a
lump, queen of the termites

or (better) speed myself up,
disguise myself in the knuckles
and purple-veined veils of old ladies,
become arthritic and genteel

or one twist further:
collapse across your
bed clutching my heart
and pull the nostalgic sheet up over
my waxed farewell smile

which would be inconvenient
but final.

In restaurants we argue
over which of us will pay for your funeral

though the real question is
whether or not I will make you immortal.

At the moment only I
can do it and so

I raise the magic fork
over the plate of beef fried rice

and plunge it into your heart.
There is a faint pop, a sizzle

and through your own split head
you rise up glowing;

the ceiling opens
a voice sings Love Is A Many-

Splendored Thing
you hang suspended above the city

in blue tights and a red cape,
your eyes flashing in unison.

The other diners regard you
some with awe, some only with boredom:

they cannot decide if you are a new weapon
or only a new advertisement.

As for me, I continue eating;
I liked you better the way you were,
but you were always ambitious.

✧

After the agony in the guest
bedroom, you lying by the
overturned bed
your face uplifted, neck propped
against the windowsill, my arm
under you, cold moon
shining down through the window

wine mist rising
around you, an almost-
visible halo

You say, Do you
love me, do you love me

I answer you:
I stretch your arms out
one to either side,
your head slumps forward.

Later I take you home
in a taxi, and you
are sick in the bathtub.

My beautiful wooden leader
with your heartful of medals
made of wood, fixing it
each time so you almost win,

you long to be bandaged
before you have been cut.
My love for you is the love
of one statue for another: tensed

and static. General, you enlist
my body in your heroic
struggle to become real:
though you promise bronze rescues

you hold me by the left ankle
so that my head brushes the ground,
my eyes are blinded,
my hair fills with white ribbons.

There are hordes of me now, alike
and paralyzed, we follow you
scattering floral tributes
under your hooves.

Magnificent on your wooden horse
you point with your fringed hand;
the sun sets, and the people all
ride off in the other direction.

Like eggs and snails you have a shell

You are widespread
and bad for the garden,
hard to eradicate

Scavenger, you feed
only on dead meat:

Your flesh by now
is pure protein,
smooth as gelatin
or the slick bellies of leeches

You are sinuous and without bones
Your tongue leaves tiny scars
the ashy texture of mildewed flowers

You thrive on smoke; you have
no chlorophyll; you move
from place to place like a disease

Like mushrooms you live in closets
and come out only at night.

✧

You want to go back
to where the sky was inside us

animals ran through us, our hands
blessed and killed according to our
wisdom, death
made real blood come out

But face it, we have been
improved, our heads float
several inches above our necks
moored to us by
rubber tubes and filled with
clever bubbles,

                our bodies
are populated with billions
of soft pink numbers
multiplying and analyzing
themselves, perfecting
their own demands, no trouble to anyone.

I love you by
sections and when you work.

Do you want to be illiterate?
This is the way it is, get used to it.

1

To understand
each other: anything
but that, & to avoid it

I will suspend my search for
germs if you will keep
your fingers off the microfilm
hidden inside my skin

2

I approach this love
like a biologist
pulling on my rubber
gloves & white labcoat

You flee from it
like an escaped political
prisoner, and no wonder

3

You held out your hand
I took your fingerprints

You asked for love
I gave you only descriptions

Please die I said
so I can write about it

A different room, this month
a worse one, where your
body with head
attached and my head with
body attached coincide briefly

I want questions and you want
only answers, but the building
is warming up, there is not much

time and time is not
fast enough for us any
more, the building sweeps
away, we are off course, we
separate, we hurtle towards each other
at the speed of sound, everything roars

we collide sightlessly and
fall, the pieces of us
mixed as disaster
and hit the pavement of this room
in a blur of silver fragments

✧

not the shore but an aquarium
filled with exhausted water and warm
seaweed
        glass clouded
with dust and algae
           tray
with the remains of dinner

smells of salt carcasses and uneaten shells

sunheat comes from wall
grating   no breeze

you sprawl across
          the bed like a marooned
starfish
      you are sand-
coloured
     on my back

your hand floats belly up

✧

You have made your escape,
your known addresses
crumple in the wind, the city
unfreezes with relief

traffic shifts back
to its routines, the swollen
buildings return to

normal, I walk believably
from house to store, nothing

remembers you but the bruises
on my thighs and the inside of my skull.

✧

Because you are never here
but always there, I forget
not you but what you look like

You drift down the street
in the rain, your face
dissolving, changing shape, the colours
running together

My walls absorb
you, breathe you forth
again, you resume
yourself, I do not recognize you

You rest on the bed
watching me watching
you, we will never know
each other any better

than we do now

Imperialist, keep off
the trees I said.

No use: you walk backwards,
admiring your own footprints.

✧

After all you are quite
ordinary: 2 arms 2 legs
a head, a reasonable
body, toes & fingers, a few
eccentricities, a few honesties
but not too many, too many
postponements & regrets but

you'll adjust to it, meeting
deadlines and other
people, pretending to love
the wrong woman some of the
time, listening to your brain
shrink, your diaries
expanding as you grow older,

growing older, of course you'll
die but not yet, you'll outlive
even my distortions of you

and there isn't anything
I want to do about the fact
that you are unhappy & sick

you aren't sick & unhappy
only alive & stuck with it.

1

These days my fingers bleed
even before I bite them

Can't play it safe, can't play
at all any more

Let's go back please
to the games, they were
more fun and less painful

2

You too have your gentle
moments, you too have
eyelashes, each of your eyes
is a different colour

in the hall light
your body stutters against
me, tentative as moths, your
skin is nervous

                I touch
your mouth, I don't
want to hurt
you any more
now than I have to

3

Waiting for news of you
which does not come, I have to
guess you

You are
in the city, climbing the stairs
already, that is you at the door

or you have gone, your last
message to me left
illegible on the mountain
road, quick
scribble of glass and blood

4

For stones, opening
is not easy

Staying closed is
less pain but

your anger finally
is more dangerous

To be picked up and thrown
(you won't stop) against

the ground, picked up
and thrown again and again

5

It's getting bad, you weren't
there again

Wire silences, you trying

to think of something you haven't
said, at least to me

Me trying to give
the impression it isn't

getting bad   at least
not yet

6

I walk the cell, open the window,
shut the window, the little
motors click
and whir, I turn on all the
taps and switches

I take pills, I drink water, I kneel

O electric lights
that shine on my suitcases and my fears

Let me stop caring
about anything but skinless
wheels and smoothly
running money

Get me out of this trap, this
body, let me be
like you, closed and useful

7

What do you expect after this?
Applause? Your name on stone?

You will have nothing
but me and in a worse way than before,

my face packed in cotton
in a white gift box, the features

dissolving and reforming so quickly
I seem only to flicker.

It would be so good if you'd
only stay up there
where I put you, I could
believe, you'd solve
most of my religious problems

you have to admit it's easier
when you're somewhere else

but today it's this
deserted mattress, music over-
heard through the end wall, you giving me
a hard time again for the fun
of it or just for

the publicity, when we leave each other
it will be so
we can say we did.

✧

yes at first you
go down smooth as
pills, all of me
breathes you in and then it's

a kick in the head, orange
and brutal, sharp jewels
hit and my
hair splinters

        the adjectives
fall away from me, no
threads left holding
me, I flake apart
layer by
layer down
quietly to the bone, my skull
unfolds to an astounded flower

regrowing the body, learning
speech again takes
days and longer
each time / too much of
this is fatal

The accident has occurred,
the ship has broken, the motor
of the car has failed, we have been
separated from the others,
we are alone in the sand, the ocean,
the frozen snow

I remember what I have to do
in order to stay alive,
I take stock of our belongings
most of them useless

I know I should be digging shelters,
killing seabirds and making
clothes from their feathers,
cutting the rinds from cacti, chewing
roots for water, scraping through
the ice for treebark, for moss

but I rest here without power
to save myself, tasting
salt in my mouth, the fact that
you won't save me

watching the mirage of us
hands locked, smiling,
as it fades into the white desert.

I touch you, straighten the sheet, you turn over
in the bed, tender
sun comes through the curtains

Which of us will survive
which of us will survive the other

✧

1

We are hard on each other
and call it honesty,
choosing our jagged truths
with care and aiming them across
the neutral table.

The things we say are
true; it is our crooked
aims, our choices
turn them criminal.

2

Of course your lies
are more amusing:
you make them new each time.

Your truths, painful and boring
repeat themselves over & over
perhaps because you own
so few of them

3

A truth should exist,
it should not be used
like this. If I love you

is that a fact or a weapon?

4

Does the body lie
moving like this, are these
touches, hairs, wet
soft marble my tongue runs over
lies you are telling me?

Your body is not a word,
it does not lie or
speak truth either.

It is only
here or not here.

Because we have no history
I construct one for you

making use of what
there is, parts of other people's
lives, paragraphs
I invent, now and then
an object, a watch, a picture
you claim as yours

(What did go on in that red
brick building with the fire
escape? Which river?)

(You said you took
the boat, you forget too much.)

I locate you on streets, in cities
I've never seen, you walk
against a background crowded
with lifelike detail

which crumbles and turns grey
when I look too closely.

Why should I need
to explain you, perhaps
this is the right place for you

The mountains in this hard
clear vacancy are blue tin
edges, you appear
without prelude midway between
my eyes and the nearest trees,

your colours bright, your
outline flattened

suspended in the air with no more
reason for occurring
exactly here than this billboard,
this highway or that cloud.

✧

At first I was given centuries
to wait in caves, in leather
tents, knowing you would never come back

Then it speeded up: only
several years between
the day you jangled off
into the mountains, and the day (it was
spring again) I rose from the embroidery
frame at the messenger's entrance.

That happened twice, or was it
more; and there was once, not so
long ago, you failed,
and came back in a wheelchair
with a moustache and a sunburn
and were insufferable.

Time before last though, I remember
I had a good eight months between
running alongside the train, skirts hitched, handing
you violets in at the window
and opening the letter; I watched
your snapshot fade for twenty years.

And last time (I drove to the airport
still dressed in my factory
overalls, the wrench
I had forgotten sticking out of the back
pocket; there you were,
zippered and helmeted, it was zero
hour, you said Be
Brave) it was at least three weeks before
I got the telegram and could start regretting.

But recently, the bad evenings
there are only seconds
between the warning on the radio and the
explosion; my hands
don't reach you

and on quieter nights
you jump up from
your chair without even touching your dinner
and I can scarcely kiss you goodbye
before you run out into the street and they shoot

✧

You refuse to own
yourself, you permit
others to do it for you:

you become slowly more public,
in a year there will be nothing left
of you but a megaphone

or you will descend through the roof
with the spurious authority of a
government official,
blue as a policeman, grey as a used angel,
having long forgotten the difference
between an annunciation and a parking ticket

or you will be slipped under
the door, your skin furred with cancelled
airmail stamps, your kiss no longer literature
but fine print, a set of instructions.

If you deny these uniforms
and choose to repossess
yourself, your future

will be less dignified, more painful, death will be sooner
(it is no longer possible
to be both human and alive): lying piled with
the others, your face and body
covered so thickly with scars
only the eyes show through.

✧

We hear nothing these days
from the ones in power

Why talk when you are a shoulder
or a vault

Why talk when you are
helmeted with numbers

Fists have many forms;
a fist knows what it can do

without the nuisance of speaking:
it grabs and smashes.

From those inside or under
words gush like toothpaste.

Language, the fist
proclaims by squeezing,
is for the weak only.

✧

You did it
it was you who started the countdown

and you conversely
on whom the demonic number
zero descended in the form of an egg-
bodied machine
coming at you like a
football or a bloated thumb

and it was you whose skin
fell off bubbling
all at once when the fence
accidentally touched you

and you also who laughed
when you saw it happen.

When will you learn
the flame and the wood / flesh
it burns are whole and the same?

You attempt merely power
you accomplish merely suffering

How long do you expect me to wait
while you cauterize your
senses, one
after another
turning yourself to an
impervious glass tower?

How long will you demand I love you?

I'm through, I won't make
any more flowers for you

I judge you as the trees do
by dying

✧

your back is rough all
over like a cat's tongue / I stroke
you lightly and you shiver

you clench yourself, withhold
even your flesh
outline / pleasure is what
you take but will not accept.

believe me, allow
me to touch you
gently, it may be the last

time / your closed eyes beat
against my fingers
I slip my hand down
your neck, rest on the pulse

you pull away

there is something in your throat that wants
to get out and you won't let it.

✧

This is a mistake,
these arms and legs
that don't work any more

Now it's broken
and no space for excuses.

The earth doesn't comfort,
it only covers up
if you have the decency to stay quiet

The sun doesn't forgive,
it looks and keeps going.

Night seeps into us
through the accidents we have
inflicted on each other

Next time we commit
love, we ought to
choose in advance what to kill.

✧

Beyond truth,
tenacity: of those
dwarf trees & mosses,
hooked into straight rock
believing the sun's lies & thus
refuting / gravity

& of this cactus, gathering
itself together
against the sand, yes tough
rind & spikes but doing
the best it can

1

In view of the fading animals
the proliferation of sewers and fears
the sea clogging, the air
nearing extinction

we should be kind, we should
take warning, we should forgive each other

Instead we are opposite, we
touch as though attacking,

the gifts we bring
even in good faith maybe
warp in our hands to
implements, to manoeuvres

2

Put down the target of me
you guard inside your binoculars,
in turn I will surrender

this aerial photograph
(your vulnerable
sections marked in red)
I have found so useful

See, we are alone in
the dormant field, the snow
that cannot be eaten or captured

3

Here there are no armies
here there is no money

It is cold and getting colder

We need each other's
breathing, warmth, surviving
is the only war
we can afford, stay

walking with me, there is almost
time / if we can only
make it as far as

the (possibly) last summer

Returning from the dead
used to be something I did well

I began asking why
I began forgetting how

✦

Spring again, can I stand it
shooting its needles into
the earth, my head, both
used to darkness

Snow on brown soil and
the squashed caterpillar
coloured liquid lawn

Winter collapses
in slack folds around
my feet / no leaves yet / loose fat

Thick lilac buds crouch for the
spurt but I
hold back

Not ready / help me
what I want from you is
moonlight smooth as
wind, long hairs of water

✧

This year I intended children
a space where I could raise
foxes and strawberries, finally
be reconciled to fur seeds & burrows

but the entrails of dead cards
are against me, foretell
it will be water, the

element that shaped
me, that I shape by
being in

      It is the blue
cup, I fill it

it is the pond again
where the children, looking from
the side of the boat, see their mother

upside down, lifesized, hair streaming
over the slashed throat
and words fertilize each other
in the cold and with bulging eyes

✧

I am sitting on the
edge of the impartial
bed, I have been turned to crystal, you enter

bringing love in the form of
a cardboard box (empty)
a pocket (empty)
some hands (also empty)

Be careful I say but
how can you
            the empty
thing comes out of your hands, it
fills the room slowly, it is
a pressure, a lack of
pressure
        Like a deep sea
creature with glass bones and wafer
eyes drawn
to the surface, I break

open, the pieces of me
shine briefly in your empty hands

✧

I see you fugitive, stumbling across the prairie,
lungs knotted by thirst, sunheat
nailing you down, all the things
after you that can be after you
with their clamps and poisoned mazes

Should I help you?
Should I make you a mirage?

My right hand unfolds rivers
around you, my left hand releases its trees,
I speak rain,
I spin you a night and you hide in it.

Now you have one enemy
instead of many.

✧

We are standing facing each other
in an eighteenth-century room
with fragile tables and mirrors
in carved frames; the curtains,
red brocade, are drawn

the doors are shut, you aren't talking,
the chandeliers aren't talking, the carpets

also remain silent.
You stay closed, your skin
is buttoned firmly around you,
your mouth is a tin decoration,
you are in the worst possible taste.

You are fake as the marble trim
around the fireplace, there is nothing
I wouldn't do to be away
from here.   I do nothing

because the light changes, the tables
and mirrors radiate from around you,
you step backwards away from me
the length of the room

holding cupped in your hands
behind your back
                        an offering
a gold word   a signal

I need more than
air, blood, it would open
everything

which you won't let me see.

✧

Sleeping in sun-
light, you occupy
me so completely

run through my brain as warm
chemicals and melted
gold, spread out wings to the
ends of my fingers
reach my heart and
stop, digging your claws in

If a bird what kind /
nothing I have ever
seen in air / you fly
through earth and water casting
a red shadow

The door wakes me, this is
your jewelled reptilian
eye in darkness next to
mine, shining feathers of
hair sift over my forehead

✧

What is it, it does not
move like love, it does
not want to know, it
does not want to stroke, unfold

it does not even want to
touch, it is more like
an animal (not
loving) a
thing trapped, you move
wounded, you are hurt, you hurt,
you want to get out, you want
to tear yourself out, I am

the outside, I am snow and
space, pathways, you gather
yourself, your muscles

clutch, you move
into me as though I
am (wrenching
your way through, this is
urgent, it is your
life) the
last chance for freedom

You are the sun
in reverse, all energy
flows into you and is
abolished; you refuse
houses, you smell of
catastrophe, I see you
blind and one-handed, flashing
in the dark, trees breaking
under your feet, you demand,
you demand

I lie mutilated beside
you; beneath us there are
sirens, fires, the people run
squealing, the city
is crushed and gutted,
the ends of your fingers bleed
from 1000 murders

Putting on my clothes
again, retreating, closing doors
I am amazed / I can continue
to think, eat, anything

How can I stop you

Why did I create you

1

I'm telling the wrong lies,
they are not even useful.

The right lies would at least
be keys, they would open the door.

The door is closed; the chairs,
the tables, the steel bowl, myself

shaping bread in the kitchen, wait
outside it.

2

That was a lie also,
I could go in if I wanted to.

Whose house is this
we both live in
but neither of us owns

How can I be expected
to find my way around

I could go in if I wanted to,
that's not the point, I don't have time,

I should be doing something
other than you.

3

What do you want from me
you who walk towards me over the long floor

your arms outstretched, your heart
luminous through the ribs

around your head a crown
of shining blood

This is your castle, this is your metal door,
these are your stairs, your

bones, you twist all possible
dimensions into your own

4

Alternate version: you advance
through the grey streets of this house,

the walls crumble, the dishes
thaw, vines grow
on the softening refrigerator

I say, leave me
alone, this is my winter,

I will stay here if I choose

You will not listen
to resistances, you cover me

with flags, a dark red
season, you delete from me
all other colours

5

Don't let me do this to you,
you are not those other people,
you are yourself

Take off the signatures, the false
bodies, this love
which does not fit you

This is not a house, there are no doors,
get out while it is
open, while you still can

6

If we make stories for each other
about what is in the room
we will never have to go in.

You say: my other wives
are in there, they are all
beautiful and happy, they love me, why
disturb them

I say: it is only
a cupboard, my collection
of envelopes, my painted
eggs, my rings

In your pockets the thin women
hang on their hooks, dismembered

Around my neck I wear
the head of the beloved, pressed
in the metal retina like a picked flower.

7

Should we go into it
together / If I go into it
with you I will never come out

If I wait outside I can salvage
this house or what is left
of it, I can keep
my candles, my dead uncles
my restrictions

but you will go
alone, either
way is loss

Tell me what it is for

In the room we will find nothing
In the room we will find each other

✧

Lying here, everything in me
brittle and pushing you away

This is not something I
wanted, I tell you

silently, not admitting
the truth of where

I am, so far
up, the sky incredible and dark

blue, each breath
a gift in the steep air

How hard even the boulders
find it to grow here

and I don't know how to accept
your freedom, I don't know

what to do with this
precipice, this joy

What do you see, I ask / my voice
absorbed by stone and outer

space / you are asleep, you see
what there is. Beside you

I bend and enter

✧

I look up, you are standing
on the other side of the window

now   your body
glimmers in the dark

room / you rise above me
smooth, chill, stone-

white / you smell of tunnels
you smell of too much time

I should have used leaves
and silver to prevent you

instead I summoned

you are not a bird you do not fly
you are not an animal you do not run

you are not a man

your mouth is nothingness
where it touches me I vanish

you descend on me like age
you descend on me like earth

✧

I can't tell you my name:
you don't believe I have one

I can't warn you this boat is falling
you planned it that way

You've never had a face
but you know that appeals to me

You are old enough to be my
skeleton: you know that also.

I can't tell you I don't want you
the sea is on your side

You have the earth's nets
I have only a pair of scissors.

When I look for you I find
water or moving shadow

There is no way I can lose you
when you are lost already.

✧

They were all inaccurate:

the hinged bronze man, the fragile man
built of glass pebbles,
the fanged man with his opulent capes and boots

peeling away from you in scales.

It was my fault but you helped,
you enjoyed it.

Neither of us will enjoy
the rest: you following me
down streets, hallways, melting
when I touch you,
avoiding the sleeves of the bargains
I hold out for you,
your face corroded by truth,

crippled, persistent. You ask
like the wind, again and again and
wordlessly, for the one forbidden thing:

love without mirrors and not for
my reasons but your own.

1

You walk towards me
carrying a new death
which is mine and no one else's;

Your face is silver
and flat, scaled like a fish

The death you bring me
is curved, it is the shape
of doorknobs, moons
glass paperweights

Inside it, snow and lethal
flakes of gold fall endlessly
over an ornamental scene,
a man and woman, hands joined and running

2

Nothing I can do will slow you
down, nothing
will make you arrive any sooner

You are serious, a gift-bearer,
you set one foot
in front of the other

through the weeks and months, across
the rocks, up from
the pits and starless
deep nights of the sea

towards firm ground and safety.

FROM

YOU ARE HAPPY

✧ ✧ ✧

NEWSREEL: MAN AND FIRING SQUAD

I

A botched job,
the blindfold slipped, he sees
his own death approaching, says No
or something, his torso jumps as the bullets hit
his nerves / he slopes down,
wrecked and not even
cleanly, roped muscles leaping, mouth open
as though snoring, the photography
isn't good either.

II

Destruction shines with such beauty

Light on his wet hair
serpents of blood jerked from the wrists

Sun thrown from the raised and lowered
rifles / debris of the still alive

Your left eye, green and lethal

III

We depart, we say goodbye

Yet each of us remains in the same place,
staked out and waiting,
it is the ground between that moves, expands,
pulling us away from each other.

No more of these closeups, this agony
taken just for the record anyway

The scenery is rising behind us
into focus, the walls
and hills are also important,

Our shattered faces retreat, we might be
happy, who can interpret
the semaphore of our bending
bodies, from a distance we could be dancing

NOVEMBER

I

This creature kneeling
dusted with snow, its teeth
grinding together, sound of old stones
at the bottom of a river

You lugged it to the barn
I held the lantern,
we leaned over it
as if it were being born.

II

The sheep hangs upside down from the rope,
a long fruit covered with wool and rotting.
It waits for the dead wagon
to harvest it.

Mournful November
this is the image
you invent for me,
the dead sheep came out of your head, a legacy:

Kill what you can't save
what you can't eat throw out
what you can't throw out bury

What you can't bury give away
what you can't give away you must carry with you,
it is always heavier than you thought.

In this yard, barnyard
I dig with a shovel

beside the temple to the goddess
of open mouths: decayed
hay, steaming
in the humid sunlight, odour
of mildewed cardboard,

filling a box with rotted dung
to feed the melons.

I dig because I hold grudges
I dig with anger
I dig because I am hungry,
the dungpile scintillates with flies.

I try to ignore my sour clothes,
the murky bread devoured
at those breakfasts, drinking orange
and black acid, butter
tasting of silt, refrigerators,
old remorse

I defend myself with the past
which is not mine,
the archaeology of manure:
this is not history, nothing ever
happened here, there were no battles

or victories: only deaths.
Witness this stained bone: pelvis
of some rodent, thrown or dragged here,
small, ferocious when cornered:

this bone is its last brittle scream,
the strict dogma of teeth.

I will wear it on a chain
around my neck: an amulet
to ward off anything

that is not a fact,
that is not food, including
symbols, monuments,
forgiveness, treaties, love.

SPRING POEM

It is spring, my decision, the earth
ferments like rising bread
or refuse, we are burning
last year's weeds, the smoke
flares from the road, the clumped stalks
glow like sluggish phoenixes / it wasn't
only my fault / birdsongs burst from
the feathered pods of their bodies, dandelions
whirl their blades upwards, from beneath
this decaying board a snake
sidewinds, chained hide
smelling of reptile sex / the hens
roll in the dust, squinting with bliss, frogbodies
bloat like bladders, contract, string
the pond with living jelly
eyes, can I be this
ruthless? I plunge
my hands and arms into the dirt,
swim among stones and cutworms,
come up rank as a fox,

restless. Nights, while seedlings
dig near my head

I dream of reconciliations
with those I have hurt
unbearably, we move still
touching over the greening fields, the future
wounds folded like seeds
in our tender fingers, days
I go for vicious walks past the charred
roadbed over the bashed stubble
admiring the view, avoiding
those I have not hurt

yet, apocalypse coiled in my tongue,
it is spring, I am searching
for the word:
         finished
         finished

so I can begin over
again, some year
I will take this word too far.

I

It's no coincidence
this is a used
furniture warehouse.

I enter with you
and become a mirror.

Mirrors
are the perfect lovers,

that's it, carry me up the stairs
by the edges, don't drop me,

that would be bad luck,
throw me on the bed

reflecting side up,
fall into me,

it will be your own
mouth you hit, firm and glassy,

your own eyes you find you
are up against   closed   closed

II

There is more to a mirror
than you looking at

your full-length body
flawless but reversed,

there is more than this dead blue
oblong eye turned outwards to you.

Think about the frame.
The frame is carved, it is important,

it exists, it does not reflect you,
it does not recede and recede, it has limits

and reflections of its own.
There's a nail in the back

to hang it with; there are several nails,
think about the nails,

pay attention to the nail
marks in the wood,

they are important too.

III

Don't assume it is passive
or easy, this clarity

with which I give you yourself.
Consider what restraint it

takes: breath withheld, no anger
or joy disturbing the surface

of the ice.
You are suspended in me

beautiful and frozen, I
preserve you, in me you are safe.

It is not a trick either,
it is a craft:

mirrors are crafty.

IV

I wanted to stop this,
this life flattened against the wall,

mute and devoid of colour,
built of pure light,

this life of vision only, split
and remote, a lucid impasse.

I confess: this is not a mirror,
it is a door

I am trapped behind.
I wanted you to see me here,

say the releasing word, whatever
that may be, open the wall.

Instead you stand in front of me
combing your hair.

V

You don't like these metaphors.
All right:

Perhaps I am not a mirror.
Perhaps I am a pool.

Think about pools.

SONGS

OF THE

TRANSFORMED

✧

PIG SONG

This is what you changed me to:
a greypink vegetable with slug
eyes, buttock
incarnate, spreading like a slow turnip,

a skin you stuff so you may feed
in your turn, a stinking wart
of flesh, a large tuber
of blood which munches
and bloats. Very well then. Meanwhile

I have the sky, which is only half
caged, I have my weed corners,
I keep myself busy, singing
my song of roots and noses,

my song of dung. Madame,
this song offends you, these grunts
which you find oppressively sexual,
mistaking simple greed for lust.

I am yours. If you feed me garbage,
I will sing a song of garbage.
This is a hymn.

For me there was no audience,
no brass music either,
only wet dust, the cheers
buzzing at me like flies,
like flies roaring.

I stood dizzied
with sun and anger,
neck muscle cut,
blood falling from the gouged shoulder.

Who brought me here
to fight against walls and blankets
and the gods with sinews of red and silver
who flutter and evade?

I turn, and my horns
gore blackness.
A mistake, to have shut myself
in this cask skin,
four legs thrust out like posts.
I should have remained grass.

The flies rise and settle.
I exit, dragged, a bale
of lump flesh.
The gods are awarded
the useless parts of my body.

For them this finish,
this death of mine is a game:
not the fact or act
but the grace with which they disguise it
justifies them.

RAT SONG

When you hear me singing
you get the rifle down
and the flashlight, aiming for my brain,
but you always miss

and when you set out the poison
I piss on it
to warn the others.

You think: *That one's too clever,
she's dangerous,* because
I don't stick around to be slaughtered
and you think I'm ugly too
despite my fur and pretty teeth
and my six nipples and snake tail.
All I want is love, you stupid
humanist. See if you can.

Right, I'm a parasite, I live off your
leavings, gristle and rancid fat,
I take without asking
and make nests in your cupboards
out of your suits and underwear.
You'd do the same if you could,

if you could afford to share
my crystal hatreds.
It's your throat I want, my mate
trapped in your throat.
Though you try to drown him
with your greasy person voice,
he is hiding / between your syllables
I can hear him singing.

In the arid sun, over the field
where the corn has rotted and then
dried up, you flock and squabble.
Not much here for you, my people,
but there would be
if
if

In my austere black uniform
I raised the banner
which decreed *Hope*
and which did not succeed
and which is not allowed.
Now I must confront the angel
who says Win,
who tells me to wave any banner
that you will follow

for you ignore me, my
baffled people, you have been through
too many theories
too many stray bullets
your eyes are gravel, skeptical,

in this hard field
you pay attention only
to the rhetoric of seed
fruit stomach elbow.

You have too many leaders
you have too many wars,
all of them pompous and small,
you resist only when you feel
like dressing up,
you forget the sane corpses . . .

I know you would like a god
to come down and feed you
and punish you. That overcoat
on sticks is not alive

there are no angels
but the angels of hunger,
prehensile and soft as gullets

Watching you
my people, I become cynical,
you have defrauded me of hope
and left me alone with politics . . .

We have been underground too long,
we have done our work,
we are many and one,
we remember when we were human

We have lived among roots and stones,
we have sung but no one has listened,
we come into the open air
at night only to love

which disgusts the soles of boots,
their leather strict religion.

We know what a boot looks like
when seen from underneath,
we know the philosophy of boots,
their metaphysic of kicks and ladders.
We are afraid of boots
but contemptuous of the foot that needs them.

Soon we will invade like weeds,
everywhere but slowly;
the captive plants will rebel
with us, fences will topple,
brick walls ripple and fall,

there will be no more boots.
Meanwhile we eat dirt
and sleep; we are waiting
under your feet.
                When we say Attack
you will hear nothing
at first.

I am the heart of a murdered woman
who took the wrong way home
who was strangled in a vacant lot and not buried
who was shot with care beneath a tree
who was mutilated by a crisp knife.
There are many of us.

I grew feathers and tore my way out of her;
I am shaped like a feathered heart.
My mouth is a chisel, my hands
the crimes done by hands.

I sit in the forest talking of death
which is monotonous:
though there are many ways of dying
there is only one death song,
the colour of mist:
it says Why   Why

I do not want revenge, I do not want expiation,
I only want to ask someone
how I was lost,
how I was lost

I am the lost heart of a murderer
who has not yet killed,
who does not yet know he wishes
to kill; who is still the same
as the others

I am looking for him,
he will have answers for me,

he will watch his step, he will be
cautious and violent, my claws
will grow through his hands
and become claws, he will not be caught.

SIREN SONG

This is the one song everyone
would like to learn: the song
that is irresistible:

the song that forces men
to leap overboard in squadrons
even though they see the beached skulls

the song nobody knows
because anyone who has heard it
is dead, and the others can't remember.

Shall I tell you the secret
and if I do, will you get me
out of this bird suit?

I don't enjoy it here
squatting on this island
looking picturesque and mythical

with these two feathery maniacs,
I don't enjoy singing
this trio, fatal and valuable.

I will tell the secret to you,
to you, only to you.
Come closer. This song

is a cry for help: Help me!
Only you, only you can,
you are unique

at last. Alas
it is a boring song
but it works every time.

SONG OF THE FOX

Dear man with the accurate mafia
eyes and dog sidekicks, I'm tired of you,
the chase is no longer fun,
the dispute for this territory
of fences and hidden caverns
will never be won, let's
leave each other alone.

I saw you as another god
I could play with in this
maze of leaves and lovely blood,
performing hieroglyphs for you
with my teeth and agile feet
and dead hens harmless and jolly
as corpses in a detective story

but you were serious,
you wore gloves and plodded,
you saw me as vermin,
a crook in a fur visor;
the fate you aim at me
is not light literature.

O you misunderstand,
a game is not a law,
this dance is not a whim,
this kill is not a rival.
I crackle through your pastures,
I make no profit / like the sun
I burn and burn, this tongue
licks through your body also

After the abrupt collision
with the blade, the Word,
I rest on the wood
block, my eyes
drawn back into their blue transparent
shells like molluscs;
I contemplate the Word

while the rest of me
which was never much under
my control, which was always
inarticulate, still runs
at random through the grass, a plea
for mercy, a single
flopping breast,

muttering about life
in its thickening red voice.

Feet and hands chase it, scavengers
intent on rape:
they want its treasures,
its warm rhizomes, enticing sausages,
its yellow grapes, its flesh
caves, five pounds of sweet money,
its juice and jellied tendons.
It tries to escape,
gasping through the neck, frantic.

They are welcome to it,

I contemplate the Word,
I am dispensable and peaceful.

The Word is an O,
outcry of the useless head,
pure space, empty and drastic,
the last word I said.
The word is No.

CORPSE SONG

I enter your night
like a darkened boat, a smuggler

These lanterns, my eyes
and heart are out

I bring you something
you do not want:

news of the country
I am trapped in,

news of your future:
soon you will have no voice

       (I resent your skin, I resent
       your lungs, your glib assumptions

Therefore sing now
while you have the choice

       (My body turned against me
       too soon, it was not a tragedy

       (I did not become
       a tree or a constellation

       (I became a winter coat the children
       thought they saw on the street corner

       (I became this illusion,
       this trick of ventriloquism

       this blind noun, this bandage
       crumpled at your dream's edge

or you will drift as I do
from head to head

swollen with words you never said,
swollen with hoarded love.

I exist in two places,
        here and where you are.

Pray for me
not as I am but as I am.

CIRCE / MUD POEMS

✦

✧

Through this forest
burned and sparse, the tines
of blunted trunks, charred branches

this forest of spines, antlers
the boat glides as if there is water

Red fireweed splatters the air
it is power, power
impinging, breaking over the seared rocks
in a slow collapse of petals

You move within range of my words
you land on the dry shore

You find what there is.

✧

Men with the heads of eagles
no longer interest me
or pig-men, or those who can fly
with the aid of wax and feathers

or those who take off their clothes
to reveal other clothes
or those with skins of blue leather

or those golden and flat as a coat of arms
or those with claws, the stuffed ones
with glass eyes; or those
hierarchic as greaves and steam-engines.

All these I could create, manufacture,
or find easily: they swoop and thunder
around this island, common as flies,
sparks flashing, bumping into each other,

on hot days you can watch them
as they melt, come apart,
fall into the ocean
like sick gulls, dethronements, plane crashes.

I search instead for the others,
the ones left over,
the ones who have escaped from these
mythologies with barely their lives;
they have real faces and hands, they think of themselves as
wrong somehow, they would rather be trees.

✧

It was not my fault, these animals
who once were lovers

it was not my fault, the snouts
and hooves, the tongues
thickening and rough, the mouths grown over
with teeth and fur

I did not add the shaggy
rugs, the tusked masks,
they happened

I did not say anything, I sat
and watched, they happened
because I did not say anything.

It was not my fault, these animals
who could no longer touch me
through the rinds of their hardening skins,
these animals dying
of thirst because they could not speak

these drying skeletons
that have crashed and litter the ground
under the cliffs, these
wrecked words.

✧

People come from all over to consult me, bringing their limbs
which have unaccountably fallen off, they don't know why, my
front porch is waist-deep in hands, bringing their blood hoarded
in pickle jars, bringing their fears about their hearts, which they
either can or can't hear at night. They offer me their pain, hoping in
return for a word, a word, any word from those they have assaulted
daily, with shovels, axes, electric saws, the silent ones, the ones
they accused of being silent because they would not speak in the
received language.

I spend my days with my head pressed to the earth, to stones,
to shrubs, collecting the few muted syllables left over; in the
evenings I dispense them, a letter at a time, trying to be fair, to the
clamouring suppliants, who have built elaborate staircases across
the level ground so they can approach me on their knees. Around
me everything is worn down, the grass, the roots, the soil, nothing
is left but the bared rock.

Come away with me, he said, we will live on a desert island. I said,
I am a desert island. It was not what he had in mind.

✧

I made no choice
I decided nothing

One day you simply appeared in your stupid boat,
your killer's hands, your disjointed body, jagged as a shipwreck,
skinny-ribbed, blue-eyed, scorched, thirsty, the usual,
pretending to be—what? a survivor?

Those who say they want nothing
want everything.
It was not this greed
that offended me, it was the lies.

Nevertheless I gave you
the food you demanded for the journey
you said you planned; but you planned no journey
and we both knew it.

You've forgotten that,
you made the right decision.
The trees bend in the wind, you eat, you rest,
you think of nothing,
your mind, you say,
is like your hands, vacant:

vacant is not innocent.

✧

There must be more for you to do
than permit yourself to be shoved
by the wind from coast
to coast to coast, boot on the boat prow
to hold the wooden body
under, soul in control

Ask at my temples
where the moon snakes, tongues of the dark
speak like bones unlocking, leaves falling
of a future you won't believe in

Ask who keeps the wind
Ask what is sacred

Don't you get tired of killing
those whose deaths have been predicted
and are therefore dead already?

Don't you get tired of wanting
to live forever?

Don't you get tired of saying Onward?

✧

You may wonder why I'm not describing the landscape for you. This island with its complement of scrubby trees, picturesque bedrock, ample weather and sunsets, lavish white sand beaches and so on. (For which I am not responsible.) There are travel brochures that do this better, and in addition they contain several very shiny illustrations so real you can almost touch the ennui of actually being here. They leave out the insects and the castaway bottles but so would I in their place; all advertisements are slanted, including this one.

You had a chance to read up on the place before you came: even allowing for distortion, you knew what you were getting into. And you weren't invited, just lured.

But why should I make excuses? Why should I describe the landscape for you? You live here, don't you? Right now I mean. See for yourself.

✧

You stand at the door
bright as an icon,

dressed in your thorax,
the forms of the indented
ribs and soft belly underneath
carved into the slick bronze
so that it fits you almost
like a real skin

You are impervious
with hope, it hardens you,
this joy, this expectation, gleams
in your hands like axes

If I allow you what you say
you want, even the day after

this, will you hurt me?

If you do I will fear you,
If you don't I will despise you

To be feared, to be despised,
these are your choices.

✦

There are so many things I want
you to have. This is mine, this
tree, I give you its name,

here is food, white like roots, red,
growing in the marsh, on the shore,
I pronounce these names for you also.

This is mine, this island, you can have
the rocks, the plants
that spread themselves flat over
the thin soil, I renounce them.

You can have this water,
this flesh, I abdicate,

I watch you, you claim
without noticing it,
you know how to take.

✧

Holding my arms down
holding my head down by the hair

mouth gouging my face
and neck, fingers groping into my flesh

> (Let go, this is extortion,
> you force my body to confess
> too fast and
> incompletely, its words
> tongueless and broken)

If I stopped believing you
this would be hate

Why do you need this?
What do you want me to admit?

✧

My face, my other faces
stretching over it like
rubber, like flowers opening
and closing, like rubber,
like liquid steel,
like steel. Face of steel.

Look at me and see your reflection.

✧

The fist, withered and strung
on a chain around my neck
wishes to hold on
to me, commands
your transformation

The dead fingers mutter
against each other, thumbs rubbing
the worn moon rituals

but you are protected,
you do not snarl
you do not change,

in the hard slot of your mouth
your teeth remain fixed,
zippered to a silver curve;
nothing rusts.

Through two holes in the leather
the discs of your eyes gleam
white as dulled quartz;
you wait

the fist stutters, gives up,
you are not visible

You unbuckle the fingers of the fist,
you order me to trust you.

✧

This is not something that can be renounced,
it must renounce.

It lets go of me
and I open like a hand
cut off at the wrist

(It is the
arm feels pain

But the severed hand
the hand clutches at freedom)

Last year I abstained
this year I devour

without guilt
which is also an art

✧

Your flawed body, sickle
scars on the chest, moonmarks, the botched knee
that nevertheless bends when you will it to

Your body, broken and put together
not perfectly, marred
by war but moving
despite that with such ease and leisure

Your body that includes everything
you have done, you have had done
to you and goes beyond it

This is not what I want
but I want this also.

✧

This story was told to me by another traveller, just passing through. It took place in a foreign country, as everything does.

When he was young he and another boy constructed a woman out of mud. She began at the neck and ended at the knees and elbows: they stuck to the essentials. Every sunny day they would row across to the island where she lived, in the afternoon when the sun had warmed her, and make love to her, sinking with ecstasy into her soft moist belly, her brown wormy flesh where small weeds had already rooted. They would take turns, they were not jealous, she preferred them both. Afterwards they would repair her, making her hips more spacious, enlarging her breasts with their shining stone nipples.

His love for her was perfect, he could say anything to her, into her he spilled his entire self. She was swept away in a sudden flood. He said no woman since then has equalled her.

Is this what you would like me to be, this mud woman? Is this what I would like to be? It would be so simple.

✧

We walk in the cedar groves
intending love, no one is here

but the suicides, returned
in the shapes of birds
with their razor-blue
feathers, their beaks like stabs, their eyes
red as the food of the dead, their single
iridescent note,
complaint or warning:

Everything dies, they say,
Everything dies.
Their colours pierce the branches.

Ignore them. Lie on the ground
like this, like the season
which is full and not theirs;

our bodies hurt them,
our mouths tasting of pears, grease,
onions, earth we eat
which was not enough for them,
the pulse under the skin, their eyes
radiate anger, they are thirsty:

Die, they whisper, Die,
their eyes consuming
themselves like stars, impersonal:

they do not care whose
blood fills the sharp trenches
where they were buried, stake through
the heart; as long
as there is blood.

✧

Not you I fear but that other
who can walk through flesh,
queen of the two dimensions.

She wears a necklace of small teeth,
she knows the ritual, she gets results,
she wants it to be like this:

Don't stand there
with your offerings of dead sheep,
chunks of wood, young children, blood,

your wet eyes, your body
gentle and taut with love,
assuming I can do nothing about it

but accept, accept, accept.
I'm not the sea, I'm not pure blue,
I don't have to take

anything you throw into me.
I close myself over, deaf as an eye,
deaf as a wound, which listens

to nothing but its own pain:
Get out of here.
Get out of here.

✧

You think you are safe at last. After your misadventures, lies, losses and cunning departures, you are doing what most veterans would like to do: you are writing a travel book. In the seclusion of this medium-sized brick building, which is ancient though not sacred any more, you disappear every morning into your white plot, filling in the dangers as you go: those with the sinister flowers who tempted you to forsake pain, the perilous and hairy eye of the groin you were forced to blind, the ones you mistook for friends, those eaters of human flesh. You add details, you colour the dead red.

I bring you things on trays, food mostly, an ear, a finger. You trust me so you are no longer cautious, you abandon yourself to your memoranda, you traverse again those menacing oceans; in the clutch of your story, your disease, you are helpless.

But it is not finished, that saga. The fresh monsters are already breeding in my head. I try to warn you, though I know you will not listen.

So much for art. So much for prophecy.

✧

When you look at nothing
what are you looking at?
Whose face floats on the water
dissolving like a paper plate?

It's the first one, remember,
the one you thought you abandoned
along with the furniture.

You returned to her after the other war
and look what happened.
Now you are wondering
whether to do it again.

Meanwhile she sits in her chair
waxing and waning
like an inner tube or a mother,
breathing out, breathing in,

surrounded by bowls, bowls, bowls,
tributes from the suitors
who are having a good time in the kitchen

waiting for her to decide
on the dialogue for this evening
which will be in perfect taste
and will include tea and sex
dispensed graciously both at once.

She's up to something, she's weaving
histories, they are never right,
she has to do them over,
she is weaving her version,

the one you will believe in,
the only one you will hear.

✧

Here are the holy birds,
grub white, with solid blood
wobbling on their heads and throats

They eat seeds and dirt, live in a shack,
lay eggs, each bursting
with a yellow sun, divine
as lunch, squeeze out,
there is only one word for it, shit,
which transforms itself to beets
or peonies, if you prefer.

We too eat
and grow fat, you aren't content
with that, you want more,
you want me to tell you
the future. That's my job,
one of them, but I advise you
don't push your luck.

To know the future
there must be a death.
Hand me the axe.

As you can see
the future is a mess,
snarled guts all over the yard
and that snakey orange eye
staring up from the sticky grass
round as a target, stopped
dead, intense as love.

✧

Now it is winter.
By winter I mean: white, silent,
hard, you didn't expect that,

it isn't supposed to occur
on this kind of island,
and it never has before

but I am the place where
all desires are fulfilled,
I mean: all desires.

Is it too cold for you?
This is what you requested,
this ice, this crystal

wall, this puzzle. You solve it.

It's the story that counts. No use telling me this isn't a story, or not the same story. I know you've fulfilled everything you promised, you love me, we sleep till noon and we spend the rest of the day eating, the food is superb, I don't deny that. But I worry about the future. In the story the boat disappears one day over the horizon, just disappears, and it doesn't say what happens then. On the island that is. It's the animals I'm afraid of, they weren't part of the bargain, in fact you didn't mention them, they may transform themselves back into men. Am I really immortal, does the sun care, when you leave will you give me back the words? Don't evade, don't pretend you won't leave after all: you leave in the story and the story is ruthless.

✧

There are two islands
at least, they do not exclude each other

On the first I am right,
the events run themselves through
almost without us,

we are open, we are closed,
we express joy, we proceed
as usual, we watch for
omens, we are sad

and so forth, it is over,
I am right, it starts again,
jerkier this time and faster,

I could say it without looking, the animals,
the blackened trees, the arrivals,

the bodies, words, it goes and goes,
I could recite it backwards.

The second I know nothing about
because it has never happened;

this land is not finished,
this body is not reversible.

We walk through a field, it is November,

the grass is yellow, tinged
with grey, the apples

are still on the trees,
they are orange, astonishing, we are standing

in a clump of weeds near the dead elms
our faces upturned, the wet flakes
falling onto our skin and melting

We lick the melted snow
from each other's mouths,
we see birds, four of them, they are gone, and

a stream not frozen yet, in the mud
beside it the track of a deer

THERE IS ONLY ONE

OF EVERYTHING

✦

I

Love is not a profession
genteel or otherwise

sex is not dentistry
the slick filling of aches and cavities

you are not my doctor
you are not my cure,

nobody has that
power, you are merely a fellow / traveller.

Give up this medical concern,
buttoned, attentive,

permit yourself anger
and permit me mine

which needs neither
your approval nor your surprise

which does not need to be made legal
which is not against a disease

but against you,
which does not need to be understood

or washed or cauterized,
which needs instead

to be said and said.
Permit me the present tense.

ii

I am not a saint or a cripple,
I am not a wound; now I will see
whether I am a coward.

I dispose of my good manners,
you don't have to kiss my wrists.

This is a journey, not a war,
there is no outcome,
I renounce predictions

and aspirins, I resign the future
as I would resign an expired passport:
picture and signature are gone
along with holidays and safe returns.

We're stuck here
on this side of the border
in this country of thumbed streets and stale buildings

where there is nothing spectacular
to see and the weather is ordinary

where *love* occurs in its pure form only
on the cheaper of the souvenirs

where we must walk slowly,
where we may not get anywhere

or anything, where we keep going,
fighting our ways, our way
not out but through.

EATING FIRE

I

Eating fire

is your ambition:
to swallow the flame down
take it into your mouth
and shoot it forth, a shout or an incandescent
tongue, a word
exploding from you in gold, crimson
unrolling in a brilliant scroll

To be lit up from within
vein by vein

To be the sun

(Taught by a sideshow man)

II

Dead man by the roadside
thrown from the overturning
truck or hit by something, a car, a bullet

On his head the hair glows,
the blood inside ignited,
short blue thorns of flame still flickering over him

Was it worth it? ask him.
(Did you save anyone?)

He gets up and walks away, the fire
growing on him like fur

III

Here the children have a custom. After the celebration of
evil they take those vacant heads that shone once with such
anguish and glee and throw them over the bridge, watching
the smash, orange, as they hit below. We were standing
underneath when you told it. People do that with them-
selves when they are finished, light scooped out. He landed
here, you said, marking it with your foot.

You wouldn't do it that way, empty, you wouldn't wait,
you would jump with the light still in you.

IV

This is your trick or miracle,
to be consumed and rise
intact, over and over, even for myths there is
a limit, the time when you accomplish
failure and return
from the fire minus your skin.

The new eyes are golden and
maniac, a bird's or lion's

Through them you see
everything, as you wished,
each object (lake, tree, woman)

transfigured with your love, shining
in its life, its pain, like waves, tears, ice,
like flesh laid open to the bone.

V

To be the sun, moving through space

distant and indifferent, giving
light of a kind for those watching

To learn how to
live this way. or not. to choose

to be also human, the body
mortal and faded, incapable of saving

itself, praying
as it falls. in its own way.

FOUR AUGURIES

I

Walking by lakeshore, feet in slush, it rains,
no grace you'd say in the dirty
ice or the goose-turd-coloured grass.

Traffic back there, illegible, passive
metal stuffed with muggy life.

Near the fence a fat man with binoculars
waddles backwards, feeding store bread
to a herd of acquiescent birds.

Bathhouse, walls patchy and scribbled over,
unredeemed, stagnant in this winter.

II

Though your body stowed in its heavy coat
is still a body: the sleeves promise me

arms, the pockets let loose their hands,
the lines on this hand hide a future

I decode only by the sense
of touch, light and urgent

the blind must rely on

III

Gulls on the breakwater, thin sounds against
the shale-grey lake. Part of us, distinct

from us, *This,* we say, taking
wet skin, smell of wet cloth, specifies,

I gather you, ear, collar, tuft of damp hair,
creases in your suddenly unfolding face

You are more than I wanted,
this is new, this greed for the real.

IV

Nothing we planned
or have understood this far. No words,
no shelter

Out here
in the open, the sky has released an owl
which drifts down and pauses

now, feathers warm snow,
hooked claws gripping the branch.

With its hooded predator's
eyes it blesses us:

mouth against throat

Omen: soft hunter

HEAD AGAINST WHITE

I

Swift curve of the lip, nose, forehead,
thrust of the bristling
jaw: a military stance.

Face closed, teeth and eyes concealed,
the body sheeted / muscles frozen shut.

Be alive, my hands
plead with you, *Be alive.*

Scar on the chin, allusion
to a minor incident, oval

dent in the skull
my fingers return to, mention with touch, cherish
as though the wound is my own.

II

The way your face
unhinges and comes apart:

confident upturned mouth, eyes
crouched in the sockets, maimed and lightblue with terror,

man on a roof's edge balancing
the moment before he topples, no can't
move, regain ground, under your weight the floor

peels back, recedes, leaving you
alone in the silent air.

It's all right. This magic fails.

No use to be the sky,
bending and watching.

III

Those times we have rumours of, arctic or alpine
when the wind and snow have stopped
at last and the rescue teams
with their tools and joyous motors

are out chasing the survivors
back from their cold refuge, hermitage
of ice to the land of sharp
colours and enforced life

Surely this is the first sign they find:
this face, rigid and fierce
with renunciation, floating up through
                            the softening white rock
like a carved long-buried god,

revealed word

IV

Under the skin's fixed surface: destroyed face
caving in on itself

No way I can walk back with you
to the country of these mutilations.

You lie here, safe, cared for, casualty
of a war that took place elsewhere,

your body replaying for you
the deserts, jungles, the smell of rotting

leaves, harsh acid scent of blood,
the mistakes, the intersections,

fact with fact, accidents
that perhaps never occurred.

Break it, I tell you, *Break
it.* Geology wins. The layer

of trite histories presses you down,
monotony of stone. Oval frame.

     V

In the mirror, face to glass face,
noon, the winter light strikes

through the window, your eyes flare, the city
burns whitely behind us. Blood flows
under the molten skin.

To move beyond the mirror's edge, discard
these scars, medals, to pronounce

your own flesh. Now

               to be this
man on fire, hands open and held
out, not empty, giving

time / From these hardened
hours, these veteran
faces, burials

to rise up living

THERE IS ONLY ONE OF EVERYTHING

Not a tree but the tree
we saw, it will never exist, split by the wind
                    and bending down
like that again, What will push out of the earth

later, making it summer, will not be
grass, leaves, repetition, there will
have to be other words. When my

eyes close language vanishes. The cat
with the divided face, half black half orange
nests in my scruffy fur coat, I drink tea,

fingers curved around the cup, impossible
to duplicate these flavours. The table
and freak plates glow softly, consuming themselves,

I look out at you and you occur
in this winter kitchen, random as trees or sentences,
entering me, fading like them, in time you will disappear

but the way you dance by yourself
on the tile floor to a worn song, flat and mournful,
so delighted, spoon waved in one hand, wisps of
                    roughened hair

sticking up from your head, it's your surprised
body, pleasure I like. I can even say it,
though only once and it won't

last: I want this. I want
this.

This is the plum season, the nights
blue and distended, the moon
hazed, this is the season of peaches

with their lush lobed bulbs
that glow in the dusk, apples
that drop and rot
sweetly, their brown skins veined as glands

No more the shrill voices
that cried *Need   Need*
from the cold pond, bladed
and urgent as new grass

Now it is the crickets
that say *Ripe Ripe*
slurred in the darkness, while the plums

dripping on the lawn outside
our window, burst
with a sound like thick syrup
muffled and slow

The air is still
warm, flesh moves over
flesh, there is no

hurry

FROM

TWO-HEADED

POEMS

✧ ✧ ✧

What comes in after a burn?
You could say nothing,

but there are flowers like dampened embers
that burst in cool white smoke

and after that, blue lights
among the leaves

that grow at the bases
of these blackened monoliths.

Before the burn, this was a forest.
Now it is something else:

a burn twists the green
eternal into singed grey

history: these discarded
stag-heads and small charred bones.

In a burn you kneel among the
reddish flowers and glowing seeds,

you give thanks as after a disaster
you were not part of,

though any burn
might have been your skin:

despite these liquid petals
against smoked rock, after a burn

your hands are never the same.

It doesn't matter how it is done,
these hints, these whispers:

whether it is some god
blowing through your head
as through a round bone
flute, or bright
stones fallen on the sand

or a charlatan, stringing you
a line with bird gut,

or smoke, or the taut hair
of a dead girl singing.

It doesn't matter what is said

but you can feel
those crystal hands, stroking
the air around your body
till the air glows white

and you are like the moon
seen from the earth, oval and gentle
and filled with light

The moon seen from the moon
is a different thing.

THE WOMAN WHO COULD NOT LIVE WITH
HER FAULTY HEART

I do not mean the symbol
of love, a candy shape
to decorate cakes with,
the heart that is supposed
to belong or break;

I mean this lump of muscle
that contracts like a flayed biceps,
purple-blue, with its skin of suet,
its skin of gristle, this isolate,
this caved hermit, unshelled
turtle, this one lungful of blood,
no happy plateful.

All hearts float in their own
deep oceans of no light,
wetblack and glimmering,
their four mouths gulping like fish.
Hearts are said to pound:
this is to be expected, the heart's
regular struggle against being drowned.

But most hearts say, I want, I want,
I want, I want. My heart
is more duplicitous,
though no twin as I once thought.
It says, I want, I don't want, I
want, and then a pause.
It forces me to listen,

and at night it is the infrared
third eye that remains open
while the other two are sleeping
but refuses to say what it has seen.

It is a constant pestering
in my ears, a caught moth, limping drum,
a child's fist beating
itself against the bedsprings:
I want, I don't want.
How can one live with such a heart?

Long ago I gave up singing
to it, it will never be satisfied or lulled.
One night I will say to it:
Heart, be still,
and it will.

I

In the house on the cliff
by the ocean, there is still a shell
bigger and lighter than your head, though now
you can hardly lift it.

It was once filled with whispers;
it was once a horn
you could blow like a shaman
conjuring the year,
and your children would come running.

You've forgotten you did that,
you've forgotten the names of the children
who in any case no longer run,
and the ocean has retreated,
leaving a difficult beach of grey stones
you are afraid to walk on.

The shell is now a cave
which opens for you alone.
It is still filled with whispers
which escape into the room,
even though you turn it mouth down.

This is your house, this is the picture
of your misty husband, these are your children, webbed
and doubled. This is the shell,

which is hard, which is still there,
solid under the hand, which mourns, which offers
itself, a narrow journey
along its hallways of cold pearl
down the cliff into the sea.

II

It is not the things themselves
that are lost, but their use and handling.

The ladder first; the beach;
the storm windows, the carpets;

The dishes, washed daily
for so many years the pattern
has faded; the floor, the stairs, your own
arms and feet whose work
you thought defined you;

The hairbrush, the oil stove
with its many failures,
the apple tree and the barrels
in the cellar for the apples,
the flesh of apples; the judging
of the flesh, the recipes
in tiny brownish writing
with the names of those who passed them
from hand to hand: Gladys,
Lorna, Winnie, Jean.

If you could only have them back
or remember who they were.

III

How little I know
about you finally:

The time you stood
in the nineteenth century
on Yonge Street, a thousand
miles from home, with a brown purse
and a man stole it.

Six children, five who lived.
She never said anything
about those births and the one death;
her mouth closed on a pain
that could neither be told nor ignored.

She used to have such a sense of fun.
Now girls, she would say
when we would tease her.
Her anger though, why
that would curl your hair,
though she never swore.
The worst thing she could say was:
Don't be foolish.

At eighty she had two teeth pulled out
and walked the four miles home
in the noon sun, placing her feet
in her own hunched shadow.

The bibbed print aprons, the shock
of the red lace dress, the pin
I found at six in your second drawer,
made of white beads, the shape of a star.
What did we ever talk about
but food, health and the weather?

Sons branch out, but
one woman leads to another.
Finally I know you
through your daughters,
my mother, her sisters,
and through myself:

Is this you, this edgy joke
I make, are these your long fingers,
your hair of an untidy bird,
is this your outraged

eye, this grip
that will not give up?

IV

Some kind of ritual
for your dwindling,
some kind of dragon, small,
benign and wooden
with two mouths to catch your soul
because it is wandering
like a lost child, lift it back safely.

But we have nothing; we say,
How is she?
Not so good, we answer,
though some days she's fine.

On other days you walk through
the door of the room in the house
where you've lived for seventy years
and find yourself in a hallway
you know you have never seen before.

Midnight, they found her
opening and closing the door
of the refrigerator:
vistas of day-old vegetables, the used bone
of an animal, and beyond that
the white ice road that leads north.

They said, Mother,
what are you doing here?

Nothing is finished
or put away, she said.
I don't know where I am.

Against the disappearance
of outlines, against
the disappearance of sounds,
against the blurring of the ears
and eyes, against the small fears
of the very old, the fear
of mumbling, the fear of dying,
the fear of falling downstairs,
I make this charm
from nothing but paper; which is good
for exactly nothing.

V

Goodbye, mother
of my mother, old bone
tunnel through which I came.

You are sinking down into
your own veins, fingers
folding back into the hand,

day by day a slow retreat
behind the disc of your face
which is hard and netted like an ancient plate.

You will flicker in these words
and in the words of others
for a while and then go out

Even if I send them,
you will never get these letters.
Even if I see you again,

I will never see you again.

She has been condemned to death by hanging. A man may escape this death by becoming the hangman, a woman by marrying the hangman. But at the present time there is no hangman; thus there is no escape. There is only a death, indefinitely postponed. This is not fantasy, it is history.

✦

To live in prison is to live without mirrors. To live without mirrors is to live without the self. She is living selflessly, she finds a hole in the stone wall and on the other side of the wall, a voice. The voice comes through darkness and has no face. This voice becomes her mirror.

✦

In order to avoid her death, her particular death, with wrung neck and swollen tongue, she must marry the hangman. But there is no hangman, first she must create him, she must persuade this man at the end of the voice, this voice she has never seen and which has never seen her, this darkness, she must persuade him to renounce his face, exchange it for the impersonal mask of death, of official death which has eyes but no mouth, this mask of a dark leper. She must transform his hands so they will be willing to twist the rope around throats that have been singled out as hers was, throats other than hers. She must marry the hangman or no one, but that is not so bad. Who else is there to marry?

✦

You wonder about her crime. She was condemned to death for stealing clothes from her employer, from the wife of her employer. She wished to make herself more beautiful. This desire in servants was not legal.

✦

She uses her voice like a hand, her voice reaches through the wall, stroking and touching. What could she possibly have said that would have convinced him? He was not condemned to death, freedom awaited him. What was the temptation, the one that worked? Perhaps he wanted to live with a woman whose life he had saved, who had seen down into the earth but had nevertheless followed him back up to life. It was his only chance to be a hero, to one person at least, for if he became the hangman the others would despise him. He was in prison for wounding another man, on one finger of the right hand, with a sword. This too is history.

✦

My friends, who are both women, tell me their stories, which cannot be believed and which are true. They are horror stories and they have not happened to me, they have not yet happened to me, they have happened to me but we are detached, we watch our unbelief with horror. Such things cannot happen to us, it is afternoon and these things do not happen in the afternoon. The trouble was, she said, I didn't have time to put my glasses on and without them I'm blind as a bat, I couldn't even see who it was. These things happen and we sit at a table and tell stories about them so we can finally believe. This is not fantasy, it is history, there is more than one hangman and because of this some of them are unemployed.

✦

He said: the end of walls, the end of ropes, the opening of doors, a field, the wind, a house, the sun, a table, an apple.

She said: nipple, arms, lips, wine, belly, hair, bread, thighs, eyes, eyes.

They both kept their promises.

✦

The hangman is not such a bad fellow. Afterwards he goes to the refrigerator and cleans up the leftovers, though he does not wipe up what he accidentally spills. He wants only the simple things: a chair, someone to pull off his shoes, someone to watch him while he talks, with admiration and fear, gratitude if possible, someone in whom to plunge himself for rest and renewal. These things can best be had by marrying a woman who has been condemned to death by other men for wishing to be beautiful. There is a wide choice.

✦

Everyone said he was a fool.
Everyone said she was a clever woman.
They used the word *ensnare*.

✦

What did they say the first time they were alone together in the same room? What did he say when she had removed her veil and he could see that she was not a voice but a body and therefore finite? What did she say when she discovered that she had left one locked room for another? They talked of love, naturally, though that did not keep them busy forever.

✦

The fact is there are no stories I can tell my friends that will make them feel better. History cannot be erased, although we can soothe ourselves by speculating about it. At that time there were no female hangmen. Perhaps there have never been any, and thus no man could save his life by marriage. Though a woman could, according to the law.

✦

He said: foot, boot, order, city, fist, roads, time, knife.

She said: water, night, willow, rope hair, earth belly, cave, meat, shroud, open, blood.

They both kept their promises.

FOUR SMALL ELEGIES

1838, 1977

I

BEAUHARNOIS

The bronze clock brought
with such care over the sea,
which ticked like the fat slow heart
of a cedar, of a grandmother,
melted and its hundred years
of time ran over the ice and froze there.

We are fixed by this frozen clock
at the edge of the winter forest.
Ten below zero.
Shouts in a foreign language
come down blue snow.

The women in their thin nightgowns
disappear wordlessly among the trees.
Here and there a shape,
a limp cloth bundle, a child
who could not keep up
lies sprawled face down in a drift
near the trampled clearing.

No one could give them clothes or shelter,
these were the orders.

We didn't hurt them, the man said,
we didn't touch them.

II

BEAUHARNOIS, GLENGARRY

Those whose houses were burned
burned houses. What else ever happens
once you start?

    While the roofs plunged
into the root-filled cellars,
they chased ducks, chickens, anything
they could catch, clubbed their heads
on rock, spitted them, singed off the feathers
in fires of blazing fences,
ate them in handfuls, charred
and bloody.

    Sitting in the snow
in those mended plaids, rubbing their numb feet,
eating soot, still hungry,
they watched the houses die like
sunsets, like their own
houses. Again

those who gave the orders
were already somewhere else,
of course on horseback.

III

BEAUHARNOIS

Is the man here, they said,
where is he?

    She didn't know, though
she called to him as they dragged her
out of the stone house by both arms
and fired the bedding.

He was gone somewhere with the other men,
he was not hanged, he came back later,
they lived in a borrowed shack,

A language is not words only,
it is the stories
that are told in it,
the stories that are never told.

He pumped himself for years
after that into her body
which had no feet
since that night, which had no fingers.
His hatred of the words
that had been done became children.

They did the best they could:
she fed them, he told them
one story only.

IV
DUFFERIN, SIMCOE, GREY

This year we are making
nothing but elegies.
Do what you are good at,
our parents always told us,
make what you know.

This is what we are making,
these songs for the dying.
You have to celebrate something.
The nets rot, the boats rot, the farms
revert to thistle, foreigners
and summer people admire the weeds
and the piles of stones dredged from the fields
by men whose teeth were gone by thirty

But the elegies are new and yellow,
they are not even made, they grow,
they come out everywhere,
in swamps, at the edges of puddles,
all over the acres
of parked cars, they are mournful
but sweet, like flowered hats
in attics we never knew we had.

We gather them, keep them in vases,
water them while our houses wither.

TWO-HEADED POEMS

"Joined Head to Head, and still alive"

ADVERTISEMENT FOR SIAMESE TWINS,
CANADIAN NATIONAL EXHIBITION, C. 1954

The heads speak sometimes singly, sometimes
together, sometimes alternately within a poem.
Like all Siamese twins, they dream of separation.

    I

Well, we felt
we were almost getting somewhere
though how that place would differ
from where we've always been, we
couldn't tell you

and then this happened,
this joke or major quake, a rift
in the earth, now everything
in the place is falling south
into the dark pit left by Cincinnati
after it crumbled.

This rubble is the future,
pieces of bureaucrats, used
bumper stickers, public names
returnable as bottles.
Our fragments made us.

What will happen to the children,
not to mention the words
we've been stockpiling for ten years now,
defining them, freezing them, storing
them in the cellar.
Anyone asked us who we were, we said
just look down there.

So much for the family business.
It was too small anyway
to be, as they say, viable.

But we weren't expecting this,
the death of shoes, fingers
dissolving from our hands,
atrophy of the tongue,
the empty mirror,
the sudden change
from ice to thin air.

    II

Those south of us are lavish
with their syllables. They scatter, we
hoard. Birds
eat their words, we eat
each other's, words, hearts, what's
the difference? In hock

up to our eyebrows, we're still
polite, god knows, to the tourists.
We make tea properly and hold the knife
the right way.

Sneering is good for you
when someone else has cornered
the tree market.

Who was it told us
so indelibly,
those who take risks
have accidents?

III

We think of you as one
big happy family, sitting around
an old pine table, trading
in-jokes, hospitable to strangers
who come from far enough away.

As for us, we're the neighbours,
we're the folks whose taste
in fences and pink iron lawn flamingoes
you don't admire.

(All neighbours are barbarians,
that goes without saying,
though you too have a trashcan.)

We make too much noise,
you know nothing about us,
you would like us to move away.

Come to our backyard, we say,
friendly and envious,
but you don't come.

Instead you quarrel
among yourselves, discussing
genealogies and the mortgage,
while the smoke from our tireless barbecues
blackens the roses.

IV

The investigator is here,
proclaiming his own necessity.
He has come to clean your heart.

Is it pure white,
or is there blood in it?

Stop this heart!
Cut this word from his mouth.
Cut this mouth.

> (Expurgation: purge.
> To purge is to clean,
> also to kill.)

For so much time, our history
was written in bones only.

Our flag has been silence,
which was mistaken for no flag,
which was mistaken for peace.

V

Is this what we wanted,
this politics, our hearts
flattened and strung out
from the backs of helicopters?

We thought we were talking
about a certain light
through the window of an empty room,
a light beyond the wet black trunks
of trees in this leafless forest
just before spring,
a certain loss.

We wanted to describe the snow,
the snow here, at the corner
of the house and orchard
in a language so precise
and secret it was not even

a code, it was snow,
there could be no translation.

To save this language
we needed echoes,
we needed to push back
the other words, the coarse ones
spreading themselves everywhere
like thighs or starlings.

No forests of discarded
crusts and torn underwear for us.
We needed guards.

Our hearts are flags now,
they wave at the end of each
machine we can stick them on.
Anyone can understand them.

They inspire pride,
they inspire slogans and tunes
you can dance to, they are redder than ever.

    VI

Despite us
there is only one universe, the sun

burns itself slowly out no matter
what you say, is that
so?   The man
up to his neck in whitehot desert
sand disagrees.

       Close your eyes now, see:
       red sun, black sun, ordinary
       sun, sunshine, sun-
       king, sunlight soap, the sun

is an egg, a lemon, a pale eye,
a lion, sun
on the beach, ice on the sun.

Language, like the mouths
that hold and release
it, is wet & living, each

word is wrinkled
with age, swollen
with other words, with blood, smoothed by the numberless
flesh tongues that have passed across it.

Your language hangs around your neck,
a noose, a heavy necklace;
each word is empire,
each word is vampire and mother.

As for the sun, there are as many
suns as there are words for sun;

false or true?

VII

Our leader
is a man of water
with a tinfoil skin.

He has two voices,
therefore two heads, four eyes,
two sets of genitals, eight
arms and legs and forty
toes and fingers.
Our leader is a spider,

he traps words.
They shrivel in his mouth,
he leaves the skins.

Most leaders speak
for themselves, then
for the people.

Who does our leader speak for?
How can you use two languages
and mean what you say in both?

No wonder our leader scuttles
sideways, melts in hot weather,
corrodes in the sea, reflects
light like a mirror,
splits our faces, our wishes,
is bitter.

Our leader is a monster
sewn from dead soldiers,
a Siamese twin.

Why should we complain?
He is ours and us,
we made him.

VIII

If I were a foreigner, as you say,
instead of your second head,
you would be more polite.

Foreigners are not there:
they pass and repass through the air
like angels, invisible
except for their cameras, and the rustle
of their strange fragrance

but we are not foreigners
to each other; we are the pressure
on the inside of the skull, the struggle
among the rocks for more room,
the shove and giveway, the grudging love,
the old hatreds.

Why fear the knife
that could sever us, unless
it would cut not skin but brain?

IX

You can't live here without breathing
someone else's air,
air that has been used to shape
these hidden words that are not yours.

This word was shut
in the mouth of a small man
choked off by the rope and gold /
red drumroll

This word was deported

This word was guttural,
buried wrapped in a leather throat
wrapped in a wolfskin

This word lies
at the bottom of a lake
with a coral bead and a kettle

This word was scrawny,
denied itself from year
to year, ate potatoes,
got drunk when possible

This word died of bad water.

Nothing stays under
forever, everyone
wants to fly, whose language
is this anyway?

You want the air
but not the words that come with it:
breathe at your peril.

These words are yours,
though you never said them,
you never heard them, history
breeds death but if you kill
it you kill yourself.

What is a traitor?

     X

This is the secret: these hearts
we held out to you, these party
hearts (our hands
sticky with adjectives
and vague love, our smiles
expanding like balloons)

these candy hearts we sent you
in the mail, a whole
bouquet of hearts, large as a country,

these hearts, like yours,
hold snipers.

A tiny sniper, one in each heart,
curled like a maggot, pallid
homunculus, pinhead, glass-eyed fanatic,
waiting to be given life.

Soon the snipers will bloom
in the summer trees, they will eat
their needle holes through your windows

(Smoke and broken leaves, up close
what a mess, wet red glass
in the zinnia border,
Don't let it come to this, we said
before it did.)

Meanwhile, we refuse
to believe the secrets of our hearts,
these hearts of neat velvet,
moral as fortune cookies.

Our hearts are virtuous, they swell
like stomachs at a wedding,
plump with goodwill.

In the evenings the news seeps in
from foreign countries,
those places with unsafe water.
We listen to the war, the wars,
any old war.

XI

Surely in your language
no one can sing, he said, one hand
in the small-change pocket.

That is a language for ordering
the slaughter and gutting of hogs, for
counting stacks of cans. Groceries
are all you are good for. Leave
the soul to us. Eat shit.

In these cages, barred crates,
feet nailed to the floor, soft
funnel down the throat,
we are forced with nouns, nouns,
till our tongues are sullen and rubbery.
We see this language always
and merely as a disease
of the mouth. Also
as the hospital that will cure us,
distasteful but necessary.

These words slow us, stumble
in us, numb us, who
can say even Open
the door, without these diffident
smiles, apologies?

Our dreams though
are of freedom, a hunger
for verbs, a song
which rises liquid and effortless,
our double, gliding beside us
over all these rivers, borders,
over ice or clouds.

Our other dream: to be mute.

Dreams are not bargains,
they settle nothing.

This is not a debate
but a duet
with two deaf singers.

It wasn't your crippled rhythm
I could not forgive, or your dark red
skinless head of a vulture

but the things you hid:
five words and my lost
gold ring, the fine blue cup
you said was broken,
that stack of faces, grey
and folded, you claimed
we'd both forgotten,
the other hearts you ate,
and all that discarded time you hid
from me, saying it never happened.

There was that, and the way
you would not be captured,
sly featherless bird, fat raptor
singing your raucous punctured song
with your talons and your greedy eye
lurking high in the molten sunset
sky behind my left cloth breast
to pounce on strangers.

How many times have I told you:
The civilized world is a zoo,
not a jungle, stay in your cage.
And then the shouts
of blood, the rage as you threw yourself
against my ribs.

As for me, I would have strangled you
gladly with both hands,
squeezed you closed, also
your yelps of joy.

Life goes more smoothly without a heart,
without that shiftless emblem,
that flyblown lion, magpie, cannibal
eagle, scorpion with its metallic tricks
of hate, that vulgar magic,
that organ the size and colour
of a scalded rat,
that singed phoenix.

But you've shoved me this far,
old pump, and we're hooked
together like conspirators, which
we are, and just as distrustful.
We know that, barring accidents,
one of us will finally
betray the other; when that happens,
it's me for the urn, you for the jar.
Until then, it's an uneasy truce,
and honour between criminals.

I

The puppet of the wolf
I have not made yet
encloses my right hand:
fur stubbles my wrists,
a tongue, avid, carnivorous,
licks between thumb and finger;
my knuckles bunch into eyes,
eyes of opaque flesh,
cunning but sightless.

The wolf is transparent, but visible:
my daughter sees it,
my right hand is the wolf.
She laughs at its comic
dance, at its roars
and piglet murders:
the bones of my left hand
squeak and crack in its grip,
in its grey teeth,
its lack of mercy.

The last house crashes down:
the wolf is on fire,
my right hand is on fire,
the wolf is gone.

II

Where has the wolf gone?
He disappeared
under the skin of my fingers,
my scalded werewolf hand,
which now, restored to normal,

slides like an ordinary
hand past the seahorse
and orange boat of the bath.

This is a miracle, there is never
any death:
the wolf comes back whenever
he is called,
unwounded and intact;
piglets jump from my thumbs.

My dying right
hand, which knots and shrinks
drier and more cynical
each year, is immortal,
briefly, and innocent.

Together with my left hand, its
enemy and prey, it chases
my daughter through the warm air,
and muted with soapsuds, lifts her
into the water.

A RED SHIRT

For Ruth

I

My sister and I are sewing
a red shirt for my daughter.
She pins, I hem, we pass the scissors
back & forth across the table.

Children should not wear red,
a man once told me.
Young girls should not wear red.

In some countries it is the colour
of death; in others passion,
in others war, in others anger,
in others the sacrifice

of shed blood. A girl should be
a veil, a white shadow, bloodless
as a moon on water; not
dangerous; she should

keep silent and avoid
red shoes, red stockings, dancing.
Dancing in red shoes will kill you.

II

But red is our colour by birth-

right, the colour of tense joy
& spilled pain that joins us

to each other. We stoop over
the table, the constant pull

of the earth's gravity furrowing
our bodies, tugging us down.

The shirt we make is stained
with our words, our stories.

The shadows the light casts
on the wall behind us multiply:

This is the procession
of old leathery mothers,

the moon's last quarter
before the blank night,

mothers like worn gloves
wrinkled to the shapes of their lives,

passing the work from hand to hand,
mother to daughter,

a long thread of red blood, not yet broken.

III

Let me tell you the story
about the Old Woman.

First: she weaves your body.
Second: she weaves your soul.

Third: she is hated & feared,
though not by those who know her.

She is the witch you burned
by daylight and crept from your home

to consult & bribe at night. The love
that tortured you, you blamed on her.

She can change her form,
and like your mother she is covered with fur.

The black Madonna
studded with miniature

arms & legs, like tin stars,
to whom they offer agony

and red candles when there is no other
help or comfort, is also her.

IV

It is January, it's raining, this grey
ordinary day. My
daughter, I would like
your shirt to be just a shirt,
no charms or fables. But fables
and charms swarm here
in this January world,
entrenching us like snow, and few
are friendly to you; though
they are strong,
potent as viruses
or virginal angels dancing
on the heads of pins,
potent as the hearts
of whores torn out
by the roots because they were thought
to be solid gold, or heavy
as the imaginary
jewels they used to split
the heads of Jews for.

It may not be true
that one myth cancels another.
Nevertheless, in a corner
of the hem, where it will not be seen,
where you will inherit
it, I make this tiny
stitch, my private magic.

    V

The shirt is finished: red
with purple flowers and pearl
buttons. My daughter puts it on,

hugging the colour
which means nothing to her
except that it is warm
and bright. In her bare

feet she runs across the floor,
escaping from us, her new game,
waving her red arms

in delight, and the air
explodes with banners.

You begin this way:
this is your hand,
this is your eye,
that is a fish, blue and flat
on the paper, almost
the shape of an eye.
This is your mouth, this is an O
or a moon, whichever
you like. This is yellow.

Outside the window
is the rain, green
because it is summer, and beyond that
the trees and then the world,
which is round and has only
the colours of these nine crayons.

This is the world, which is fuller
and more difficult to learn than I have said.
You are right to smudge it that way

with the red and then
the orange: the world burns.

Once you have learned these words
you will learn that there are more
words than you can ever learn.
The word *hand* floats above your hand
like a small cloud over a lake.
The word *hand* anchors
your hand to this table,
your hand is a warm stone
I hold between two words.

This is your hand, these are my hands, this is the world,
which is round but not flat and has more colours
than we can see.

It begins, it has an end,
this is what you will
come back to, this is your hand.

TRUE STORIES

✧ ✧ ✧

TRUE STORIES

I

Don't ask for the true story;
why do you need it?

It's not what I set out with
or what I carry.

What I'm sailing with,
a knife, blue fire,

luck, a few good words
that still work, and the tide.

II

The true story was lost
on the way down to the beach, it's something

I never had, that black tangle
of branches in a shifting light,

my blurred footprints
filling with salt

water, this handful
of tiny bones, this owl's kill;

a moon, crumpled papers, a coin,
the glint of an old picnic,

the hollows made by lovers
in sand a hundred

years ago: no clue.

III

The true story lies
among the other stories,

a mess of colours, like jumbled clothing
thrown off or away,

like hearts on marble, like syllables, like
butchers' discards.

The true story is vicious
and multiple and untrue

after all. Why do you
need it? Don't ever

ask for the true story.

The sea sucks at its own
edges, in and out with the moon.
Tattered brown fronds
(shredded nylon stockings,
feathers, the remnants of hands)
wash against my skin.

As for the crab, she's climbed
a tree and sticks herself
to the bark with her adroit
spikes; she jerks
her stalked eyes at me, seeing

a meat shadow,
food or a predator.
I smell the pulp
of her body, faint odour
of rotting salt,
as she smells mine,
working those Martian palps:

seawater in leather.
I'm a category, a noun
in a language not human,
infra-red in moonlight,
a tidal wave in the air.

Old fingernail, old mother,
I'm up to scant harm
tonight; though you don't care,

you're no one's metaphor,
you have your own paths
and rituals, frayed snails
and soaked nuts, waterlogged sacks
to pick over, soggy chips and crusts.

The beach is all yours, wordless
and ripe once I'm off it,
wading towards the moored boats
and blue lights of the dock.

POSTCARD

I'm thinking about you. What else can I say?
The palm trees on the reverse
are a delusion; so is the pink sand.
What we have are the usual
fractured coke bottles and the smell
of backed-up drains, too sweet,
like a mango on the verge
of rot, which we have also.
The air clear sweat, mosquitoes
& their tracks; birds, blue & elusive.

Time comes in waves here, a sickness, one
day after the other rolling on;
I move up, it's called
awake, then down into the uneasy
nights but never
forward. The roosters crow
for hours before dawn, and a prodded
child howls & howls
on the pocked road to school.
In the hold with the baggage
there are two prisoners,
their heads shaved by bayonets, & ten crates
of queasy chicks. Each spring
there's a race of cripples, from the store
to the church. This is the sort of junk
I carry with me; and a clipping
about democracy from the local paper.

Outside the window
they're building the damn hotel,
nail by nail, someone's
crumbling dream. A universe that includes you
can't be all bad, but
does it? At this distance

you're a mirage, a glossy image
fixed in the posture
of the last time I saw you.
Turn you over, there's the place
for the address. Wish you were
here. Love comes
in waves like the ocean, a sickness which goes on
& on, a hollow cave
in the head, filling & pounding, a kicked ear.

Nothing like love to put blood
back in the language,
the difference between the beach and its
discrete rocks & shards, a hard
cuneiform, and the tender cursive
of waves; bone & liquid fishegg, desert
& saltmarsh, a green push
out of death. The vowels plump
again like lips or soaked fingers, and the fingers
themselves move around these
softening pebbles as around skin. The sky's
not vacant and over there but close
against your eyes, molten, so near
you can taste it. It tastes of
salt. What touches
you is what you touch.

FROM NOTES TOWARDS A POEM THAT CAN
NEVER BE WRITTEN

FLYING INSIDE YOUR OWN BODY

Your lungs fill & spread themselves,
wings of pink blood, and your bones
empty themselves and become hollow.
When you breathe in you'll lift like a balloon
and your heart is light too & huge,
beating with pure joy, pure helium.
The sun's white winds blow through you,
there's nothing above you,
you see the earth now as an oval jewel,
radiant & seablue with love.

It's only in dreams you can do this.
Waking, your heart is a shaken fist,
a fine dust clogs the air you breathe in;
the sun's a hot copper weight pressing straight
down on the thick pink rind of your skull.
It's always the moment just before gunshot.
You try & try to rise but you cannot.

THE ARREST OF THE STOCKBROKER

They broke the hands of the musician
and when despite that he would not stop singing
they shot him. That was expected.

You expected the poet hung upside down
by one foot with clothesline: in your head
you coloured his hair green. Art needs martyrs.

And the union leader with electrodes
clipped to the more florid
parts of his body, wired like
an odd zoological diagram:
if you don't keep your mouth shut
they'll choose the noise
you emit. Anyone knows that.
In some way he wanted it.

Reading the papers, you've seen it all:
the device for tearing out fingernails,
the motors, the accessories,
what can be done with the common pin.
Not to mention the wives and children.

Who needs these stories
that exist in the white spaces
at the edges of the page,
banal and without shape, like snow?

You flip to the travel ads; you're unable
to shake the concept of tragedy,
that what one gets
is what's deserved, more
or less; that there's a plot,
and innocence is merely
not to act.

Then suddenly you're in there,
in this mistake, this stage, this box,
this war grinding across
your body. You can't believe it.

Not only that, he's in here with you,
the man with the documents,
the forms, the stamps, the ritual prayers, the seals,
red & silver, and the keys, the signatures.

Those are his screams you hear,
the man you were counting on
to declare you legitimate:
the man you were always counting on
to get you out.

FRENCH COLONIAL

For Son Mitchell

This was a plantation once,
owned by a Frenchman. The well survives,
filled now with algae, heartcoloured
dragonflies, thin simmer of mosquitoes.

Here is an archway, grown over
with the gross roots of trees,
here's a barred window,
a barn or prison.
Fungus blackens the walls
as if they're burned, but no need:
thickening vines lick over
and through them, a slow
green fire. Sugar,
it was then. Now there are rows
of yellowing limes, the burrows
of night crabs. Five hundred yards
away, seared women in flowered dresses
heap plates at the buffet.
We'll soon join them.
The names of the bays:
Hope, Friendship and Industry.

The well is a stone hole
opening out of darkness,
drowned history. Who knows
what's down there? How many
spent lives, killed muscles.
It's the threshold of an unbuilt

house. We sit on the rim
in the sun, talking
of politics. You could still
drink the water.

EARTH

It isn't winter that brings it
out, my cowardice,
but the thickening summer I wallow in
right now, stinking of lilacs, green
with worms & stamens duplicating themselves
each one the same

I squat among rows of seeds & imposters
and snout my hand into the juicy dirt:
charred chicken bones, rusted nails,
dogbones, stones, stove ashes.
Down there is another hand, yours, hopeless,
down there is a future

in which you're a white white picture
with a name I forgot to write
underneath, and no date,

in which you're a suit
hanging with its stubs of sleeves
in a cupboard in a house
in a city I've never entered,

a missed beat in space
which nevertheless unrolls itself
as usual. As usual:
that's why I don't want to go on with this.

(I'll want to make a hole in the earth
the size of an implosion, a leaf, a dwarf
star, a cave
in time that opens back & back into
absolute darkness and at last

into a small pale moon of light
the size of a hand,
I'll want to call you out of the grave
in the form of anything at all)

This is a word we use to plug
holes with. It's the right size for those warm
blanks in speech, for those red heart-
shaped vacancies on the page that look nothing
like real hearts. Add lace
and you can sell
it. We insert it also in the one empty
space on the printed form
that comes with no instructions. There are whole
magazines with not much in them
but the word *love,* you can
rub it all over your body and you
can cook with it too. How do we know
it isn't what goes on at the cool
debaucheries of slugs under damp
pieces of cardboard? As for the weed-
seedlings nosing their tough snouts up
among the lettuces, they shout it.
Love! Love! sing the soldiers, raising
their glittering knives in salute.

Then there's the two
of us. This word
is far too short for us, it has only
four letters, too sparse
to fill those deep bare
vacuums between the stars
that press on us with their deafness.
It's not love we don't wish
to fall into, but that fear.
This word is not enough but it will
have to do. It's a single
vowel in this metallic
silence, a mouth that says

O again and again in wonder
and pain, a breath, a finger-
grip on a cliffside. You can
hold on or let go.

SUNSET II

Sunset, now that we're finally in it
is not what we thought.

Did you expect this violet black
soft edge to outer space, fragile as blown ash
and shuddering like oil, or the reddish
orange that flows into
your lungs and through your fingers?
The waves smooth mouthpink light
over your eyes, fold after fold.
This is the sun you breathe in,
pale blue. Did you
expect it to be this warm?

One more goodbye,
sentimental as they all are.
The far west recedes from us
like a mauve postcard of itself
and dissolves into the sea.

Now there's a moon,
an irony. We walk
north towards no home,
joined at the hand.

I'll love you forever,
I can't stop time.

This is you on my skin somewhere
in the form of sand.

I would like to watch you sleeping,
which may not happen.
I would like to watch you,
sleeping. I would like to sleep
with you, to enter
your sleep as its smooth dark wave
slides over my head

and walk with you through that lucent
wavering forest of bluegreen leaves
with its watery sun & three moons
towards the cave where you must descend,
towards your worst fear

I would like to give you the silver
branch, the small white flower, the one
word that will protect you
from the grief at the centre
of your dream, from the grief
at the centre. I would like to follow
you up the long stairway
again & become
the boat that would row you back

carefully, a flame
in two cupped hands
to where your body lies
beside me, and you enter
it as easily as breathing in

I would like to be the air
that inhabits you for a moment
only. I would like to be that unnoticed
& that necessary.

FROM

INTERLUNAR

✧ ✧ ✧

SNAKE POEMS

✦

LESSON ON SNAKES

Pinned down, this one
opens its mouth as wide as it can
showing fangs and a throat
like the view down a pink lily,
double tongue curved out like stamens.

The lilies do it to keep
from being eaten, this dance of snakes

and the snakes do it to keep from being
eaten also. Since they cannot talk:

the snake is a mute
except for the sound like steam
escaping from a radiator
it makes when cornered:
something punctured and leaking.

This one is green and yellow,
striped like a moose maple.
Sweetly and with grace it hunts
a glimpse, a rustle
among the furry strawberries.

It's hardly
the devil in your garden
but a handy antidote to mice

and yet you'd batter it
with that hoe or crowbar
to a twist of slack rope:

a bad answer
to anything that gets in
what you think is your way.

I present the glass snake
which is supposed to break when stepped on
but doesn't. One more lie about snakes,

nor is it transparent. Nothing
could be more opaque. Watch it
there as it undulates over the sand,
a movement of hips in a tight skirt.
You remember the legends
of snakes which were changed to women
and vice versa. Another lie.

Other lies about snakes:
that they cause thunder,
that they won't cross ropes,
that they travel in pairs:
(even when together
for warmth at night or in winter,
snakes are alone)

Swaying up from coiled baskets
they move as if to music,
but snakes cannot hear music.
The time they keep is their own.

BAD MOUTH

There are no leaf-eating snakes.
All are fanged and gorge on blood.
Each one is a hunter's hunter,
nothing more than an endless gullet
pulling itself on over the still-alive prey
like a sock gone ravenous, like an evil glove,
like sheer greed, lithe and devious.

Puff adder buried in hot sand
or poisoning the toes of boots,
for whom killing is easy and careless
as war, as digestion,
why should you be spared?

And you, *Constrictor constrictor,*
sinuous ribbon of true darkness,
one long muscle with eyes and an anus,
looping like thick tar out of the trees
to squeeze the voice from anything edible,
reducing it to scales and belly,

And you, pit viper
with your venomous pallid throat
and teeth like syringes
and your nasty radar
homing in on the deep red shadow
nothing else knows it casts . . .
Shall I concede these deaths?

Between us there is no fellow feeling,
as witness: a snake cannot scream.
Observe the alien
chainmail skin, straight out
of science fiction, pure
shiver, pure Saturn.

Those who can explain them
can explain anything.

Some say they're a snarled puzzle
only gasoline and a match can untangle.
Even their mating is barely sexual,
a romance between two lengths
of cyanide-coloured string.
Despite their live births and squirming nests
it's hard to believe in snakes loving.

Alone among the animals
the snake does not sing.
The reason for them is the same
as the reason for stars, and not human.

I too have taken the god into my mouth,
chewed it up and tried not to choke on the bones.
Rattlesnake it was, panfried
and good too though a little oily.

(Forget the phallic symbolism:
two differences:
snake tastes like chicken,
and who ever credited the prick with wisdom?)

All peoples are driven
to the point of eating their gods
after a time: it's the old greed
for a plateful of outer space, that craving for darkness,
the lust to feel what it does to you
when your teeth meet in divinity, in the flesh,
when you swallow it down
and you can see with its own cold eyes,
look out through murder.

This is a lot of fuss to make about mere lunch:
metaphysics with onions.
The snake was not served with its tail in its mouth
as would have been appropriate.
Instead the cook nailed the skin to the wall,
complete with rattles, and the head was mounted.
It was only a snake after all.

(Nevertheless, the authorities are agreed:
God is round.)

The white snake is to be found, says legend,
at the dark of the moon,
by the forks of roads, under three-leaved trees,
at the bottoms of unsounded lakes.

It looks like water
freezing. It has no eyes.
It lays quartz eggs and foretells the future.

If you can find it and eat it
then you will understand
the languages of the animals.

There was a man who tried it.
He hunted, caught, transformed
the sacred body of living snow
into raw meat, cut into it, swallowed.

Then sound poured over him
like a wall breaking, like a disaster:

He went blind in an instant.
Light rose in him
filling his mouth like blood,
like earth in the mouth of a man buried.

Human speech left him.
For the rest of his life, emptied and mute
he could do nothing but listen
to the words, words around him everywhere like rain falling.

Beware of the white snake, says the story.
Choose ignorance.

(There are no white snakes in nature.)

The snake is one name of God,
my teacher said:
All nature is a fire
we burn in and are
renewed, one skin
shed and then another.

To talk with the body
is what the snake does, letter
after letter formed on the grass,
itself a tongue, looping its earthy hieroglyphs,
the sunlight praising it
as it shines there on the doorstep,
a green light blessing your house.

This is the voice
you could pray to for the answers
to your sickness:
leave it a bowl of milk,
watch it drink

You do not pray, but go for the shovel,
old blood on the blade

But pick it up and you would hold
the darkness that you fear
turned flesh and embers,
cool power coiling into your wrists
and it would be in your hands
where it always has been.

This is the nameless one
giving itself a name,
one among many

and your own name as well.

You know this and still kill it.

INTERLUNAR

BEDSIDE

You sit beside the bed
in the *extremis* ward, holding your father's feet
as you have not done since you were a child.
You would hold his hands, but they are strapped down,
emptied at last of power.

He can see, possibly, the weave of the sheet
that covers him from chest to ankles;
he does not wish to.

He has been opened. He is at the mercy.

You hold his feet,
not moving. You would like
to drag him back. You remember
how you have judged each other
in silence, relentlessly.

You listen intently, as if for a signal,
to the undersea ping of the monitors,
the waterlogged lungs breathed into by machines,
the heart, wired for sound
and running too quickly in the stuck body,

the murderous body, the body
itself stalled in a field of ice
that spreads out endlessly under it,
the snowdrifts tucked by the wind around
the limbs and torso.

Now he is walking
somewhere you cannot follow,
leaving no footprints.
Already in this whiteness
he casts no shadow.

LUNCHTIME DURING A PEAK YEAR
IN THE YELLOWJACKET CYCLE

Right now we live in tents
and wake in the orange light and tar
smell of canvas heating
in the sun. When it rains we play cards.
We eat our foods
in the order in which they will otherwise
rot, the hardiest last.

Today the lake simmers,
bright as the tin plates
we wash in it. The wasps are thick,
lured by the chance of perishing
and spoilage; they flounder
in the enamel cups of smoky
tea, perch on the damp paper
the meat was wrapped in before it melted,
the peaches in sweet syrup
tasting of metal,
the spoons raised halfway to our mouths.
They saw and gorge themselves and stagger
into the air, dizzy with blood and sugar.

The stew muscle in its juices
ferments over the fire.
A wasp falls into the pot,
flutters like a tinsel heart
and is cooked, adding its tiny hurt.

Look before you eat, says my mother
as she stoops and ladles.
Her nomadic children ignore her.
Every year she is shorter
and we are more oblivious.
Already we are beyond her power

to save us from even small disasters.
We have our own purposes.
We think we can do what we want.

This is the summer I am going to devour
everything I can dig up or strangle,
each muddy clam and bitter stem,
looking it up in the book first.

I squat, the gold wasps crawling
harmless over my bare arms and leathery
toes, thinking about my secret meals,
nearly savage and single-
minded and living
off the land, stirring a purple
swampy cattail soup
in a tomato can on a hot stone
and burning it, ferocious
with hunger for every untried
food, dazed by the sunlight
and abundance, knowing nothing about death.

The saints cannot distinguish
between being with other people and being
alone: another good reason for becoming one.

They live in trees and eat air.
Staring past or through us, they see
things which we would call not there.
We on the contrary see them.

They smell of old fur coats
stored for a long time in the attic.
When they move they ripple.
Two of them passed here yesterday,
filled and vacated and filled
by the wind, like drained pillows
blowing across a derelict lot,
their twisted and scorched feet
not touching the ground,
their feathers catching in thistles.
What they touched emptied of colour.

Whether they are dead or not
is a moot point.
Shreds of them litter history,
a hand here, a bone there:
is it suffering or goodness
that makes them holy,
or can anyone tell the difference?

Though they pray, they do not pray
for us. Prayers peel off them
like burned skin healing.
Once they tried to save something,
others or their own souls.
Now they seem to have no use,

like the colours on blind fish.
Nevertheless they are sacred.

They drift through the atmosphere,
their blue eyes sucked dry
by the ordeal of seeing,
exuding gaps in the landscape as water
exudes mist. They blink
and reality shivers.

In the warm dusk over the exhausted trees
outside the farmhouse, in the scent
of soft brick and hot tin,

weeding among the white-pink peonies,
their sugary heads heavy and swollen,
I can hear them breathing out
and then out again, as if giving up.

It's June, the month when the dead
are least active though most hungry

and I'm too close to the ground, to those
who have faded and merged, too close
to contagion. Hidden in the border somewhere
near, a bone sings of betrayal.

My fingers are wet with bruised
green stems and dewfall.
In this season of opening out,
there is something I want closed.

The sun sinks and the body darkens
from within: I can see the light going out of my hands.

I doubt that I ever loved you.
I believe I have chosen peace.

Think of this as the dormant phase
of a disease.

KEEP

I know that you will die
before I do.

Already your skin tastes faintly
of the acid that is eating through you.

None of this, none of this is true,
no more than a leaf is botany,

along this avenue of old maples
the birds fall down through the branches
as the long slow rain of small bodies
falls like snow through the darkening sea,

wet things in turn move up out of the earth,
your body is liquid in my hands, almost
a piece of solid water.

Time is what we're doing,
I'm falling into the flesh,
into the sadness of the body
that cannot give up its habits,
habits of the hands and skin.

I will be one of those old women
with good bones and stringy necks
who will not let go of anything.

You'll be there. You'll keep
your distance,
the same one.

The skin seethes in the heat
which roars out from the sun, wave after tidal wave;
the sea is flat and hot and too bright,
stagnant as a puddle,
edged by a beach reeking of shit.
The city is like a city
bombed out and burning;
the smell of smoke is everywhere,
drifting from the mounds of rubble.
Now and then a new tower,
already stained, lifts from the tangle;
the cars stall and bellow.
From the trampled earth rubbish erupts
and huts of tin and warped boards
and cloth and anything scavenged.
Everything is the colour of dirt
except the kites, red and purple,
three of them, fluttering cheerfully
from a slope of garbage,
and the women's dresses, cleaned somehow,
vaporous and brilliant, and the dutiful
white smiles of the child beggars
who kiss your small change
and press it to their heads and hearts.

Uncle, they call you. *Mother.*
I have never felt less motherly.
The moon is responsible for all this,
goddess of increase
and death, which here are the same.
Why try to redeem
anything? In this maze
of condemned flesh without beginning or end
where the pulp of the body steams and bloats
and spawns and multiplies itself
the wise man chooses serenity.

Here you are taught the need to be holy,
to wash a lot and live apart.
Burial by fire is the last mercy:
decay is reserved for the living.

The desire to be loved is the last illusion:
Give it up and you will be free.

BOMBAY, 1982

You walked in front of me,
pulling me back out
to the green light that had once
grown fangs and killed me.

I was obedient, but
numb, like an arm
gone to sleep; the return
to time was not my choice.

By then I was used to silence.
Though something stretched between us
like a whisper, like a rope:
my former name,
drawn tight.
You had your old leash
with you, love you might call it,
and your flesh voice.

Before your eyes you held steady
the image of what you wanted
me to become: living again.
It was this hope of yours that kept me following.

I was your hallucination, listening
and floral, and you were singing me:
already new skin was forming on me
within the luminous misty shroud
of my other body; already
there was dirt on my hands and I was thirsty.

I could see only the outline
of your head and shoulders,
black against the cave mouth,
and so could not see your face
at all, when you turned

and called to me because you had
already lost me. The last
I saw of you was a dark oval.
Though I knew how this failure
would hurt you, I had to
fold like a grey moth and let go.

You could not believe I was more than your echo.

He is here, come down to look for you.
It is the song that calls you back,
a song of joy and suffering
equally: a promise:
that things will be different up there
than they were last time.

You would rather have gone on feeling nothing,
emptiness and silence; the stagnant peace
of the deepest sea, which is easier
than the noise and flesh of the surface.

You are used to these blanched dim corridors,
you are used to the king
who passes you without speaking.

The other one is different
and you almost remember him.
He says he is singing to you
because he loves you,

not as you are now,
so chilled and minimal: moving and still
both, like a white curtain blowing
in the draft from a half-opened window
beside a chair on which nobody sits.

He wants you to be what he calls real.
He wants you to stop light.
He wants to feel himself thickening
like a treetrunk or a haunch
and see blood on his eyelids
when he closes them, and the sun beating.

This love of his is not something
he can do if you aren't there,
but what you knew suddenly as you left your body
cooling and whitening on the lawn

was that you love him anywhere,
even in this land of no memory,
even in this domain of hunger.
You hold love in your hand, a red seed
you had forgotten you were holding.

He has come almost too far.
He cannot believe without seeing,
and it's dark here.
Go back, you whisper,

but he wants to be fed again
by you. O handful of gauze, little
bandage, handful of cold
air, it is not through him
you will get your freedom.

ONE SPECIES OF LOVE, AFTER A PAINTING
BY HIERONYMUS BOSCH

In the foreground there are a lot of stones,
each one painted singly
and in detail.

There is a man, sitting down.
Behind the man is a hill,
shaped like a mound burial
or a pudding,
with scrubby bushes, the leaves glazed
by the serene eye-colour of the sky.
In the middle distance, an invisible line
beyond which things become
abruptly bluer.

At the man's feet there is a lion,
plush-furred and blunted,
and in the right foreground, a creature
part bird, part teapot,
part lizard and part hat
is coming out of an eggshell.

The man himself, in his robe
the muted pink of the ends of fingers
is gazing up at the halfsized
woman who is suspended
in the air over his head.

She has wings, but they aren't moving.
She's blue, like the background,
denoting holiness or distance
or perhaps lack of a body.

She holds one hand in a gesture
of benediction which is a little wooden.
The other hand points to the ground.

There is no sound in this picture,
light but no shadows.
The stones keep still.
The surface is clear
and without texture.

You know the landscape: in the distance
three low hills, bare of snow.

In the foreground the willow grove
along the unmoving river
not icebound. Snow in the shadows though.
A diffused light that is not the sun.

Here and there, the young girls
in their white dresses made of paper
not written on.
No one is here willingly.
None are mourners.

Each stays under a separate tree,
sitting or standing as if
aimless. It was not
an end they wanted but more life.

The near one crouches on the chilled
sand, knees to belly,
holding in her hands a plain stone
she turns over and over,
puzzled, searching for the cut in it
where the blood ran out.

The tree arching above her
is dead, like everything
here. Nevertheless it sways, although there is
no wind, quickening and shaking out
for her its thin leaves and small green flowers,

which has never happened before,
which happens every day,
which she does not notice.

He would like not to kill. He would like
what he imagines other men have,
instead of this red compulsion. Why do the women
fail him and die badly? He would like to kill them gently,
finger by finger and with great tenderness, so that
at the end they would melt into him
with gratitude for his skill and the final pleasure
he still believes he could bring them
if only they would accept him,
but they scream too much and make him angry.
Then he goes for the soul, rummaging
in their flesh for it, despotic with self-pity,
hunting among the nerves and the shards
of their faces for the one thing
he needs to live, and lost
back there in the poplar and spruce forest
in the watery moonlight, where his young bride,
pale but only a little frightened,
her hands glimmering with his own approaching
death, gropes her way towards him
along the obscure path, from white stone
to white stone, ignorant and singing,
dreaming of him as he is.

The villagers are out hunting for you.
They have had enough of potions
for obtaining love: they do not want love
this year, the crops were scant, a bad wind
came with the fall mists and they want you.

Already they have burned your house,
broken your mirror
in which they used to glimpse over their shoulders
the crescent moon and the face
of the one desired,
kicked the charred bedding apart
looking for amulets, gutted your cats.

By night you walk in the fields, fending off
the voices that rustle in the air
around you, wading streams
to kill your smell,
or creep into the barns to steal milk
and the turnips the pigs eat.
By day you hide,
digging yourself in under the hedges,
your dress becoming the colour of ashes.
Praying to the rain to save you.

Through the smooth grey tree-trunks there are fragments
of coats, the red wool
sashes, whistles rallying the dogs,
drifting towards you through the leaves falling
like snow, like pestilence.

Of the men who will stand around
the peeled stake dug into a pit,
bundles of sticks and dried reeds piled
nearby, the mud caked on their bootsoles,

crooking their fingers to ward you off,
at the same time joking about
your slashed breasts and the avid
heat to come, there is not one

who has not run his hands over your skin
in stealth, yours or your shadow's,
not one who has not straddled you
in the turned furrows, begging for increase.

What you will see: the sun, for the last time.
The tree-strewn landscape gathering itself
around you; the blighted meadows.
The dark ring of men whose names
you know, and their bodies
you remember as nameless, luminous.
The children, on the edges

of the circle, twisting on the ground,
arms uplifted and spread, mouths open, playing
at being you. In the distance, the wives
in their flowered shawls and thick decorous
skirts, hurrying from their houses
with little pierced copper
bowls in their hands, as if offering food
at a feast, bringing the embers.

Sometimes there is an idea
so pure it is without mercy.

It sweeps over the wet fields
where rice is planted by women
in bare feet and pink skirts
and hits the jungles like a blade
of hard light. Love
in the abstract is deadly.

Some died for embracing
each other, some for speaking,
some for remaining silent,
some for remaining.
The wells filled up. After a time
nobody bothered burying.

In a jungle this hot
the afterlife happens quickly
and tenderly. Ants flow like water.
Week-old bodies
are already without flesh and eyes.
Even so many of them.
Tendrils grow around them
as if forgiving them.
Vines break out their raucous flowers
despite them.

The ruinous huts, the parts
of children gnawed by cats, the cooking
fires left smouldering, the cairns
of bones arranged so neatly.
In the service
of the word.

I would say the stones
cry out, except they don't.
Nothing cries out. The light falls on all of this
equally. Fear and memory
work their way down into the earth
and lie fallow.

Whether he will go on singing
or not, knowing what he knows
of the horror of this world:

He was not wandering among meadows
all this time. He was down there
among the mouthless ones, among
those with no fingers, those
whose names are forbidden,
those washed up eaten into
among the grey stones
of the shore where nobody goes
through fear. Those with silence.

He has been trying to sing
love into existence again
and he has failed.

Yet he will continue
to sing, in the stadium
crowded with the already dead
who raise their eyeless faces
to listen to him; while the red flowers
grow up and splatter open
against the walls.

They have cut off both his hands
and soon they will tear
his head from his body in one burst
of furious refusal.
He foresees this. Yet he will go on
singing, and in praise.
To sing is either praise
or defiance. Praise is defiance.

THE SIDEWALK

We're hand in hand along
any old street, by the lake this time, and laughing
too at some joke we've
made and forgotten, and the sun
shines or it's raining, lunch after lunch, dinner
after dinner. You could see it
as one thing after another. Where
are we going? It looks like
nowhere; though we're going
where love goes finally, we're
going under. But not
yet, we're still
incarnate, though the trees break
into flame, blaze up, shed
in one gasp, turn to ash, each thing
burns over and over and we will
too, even the lake's
on fire now, it's evening and the sidewalk
fills with blue light, you can see down
through it, we walk on
water for a split
second before faith lapses and we let go
of each other also. Everything's
brighter just before, and it's
just before always.

THE WHITE CUP

What can I offer you, my hands held open,
empty except for my hands?

There is nothing to be afraid of,
you don't need my blessing.

As for the pigeons and the cedars
fading at dusk and emerging in early morning,
they can get along maybe
even better without me noticing them.

Coming back from a long illness
you can see how the white cup, the nasturtiums
on the porch, everything shines
not flagrantly as it did during your fever
but only the way it does.

This is the one thing I wanted to give you,
this quiet shining
which is a constant entering,
a going into

THE SKELETON, NOT AS AN IMAGE OF DEATH

Your flesh moves under my fingers

and I remember *flesh* and *fingers,* as a child holding
the head of a flashlight cupped in my fist
in a dark room, seeing with such delight
the outlines of my own hand's
lucent skeleton, swathed in the red glow
of the blood clouded within

and this is how I hold
you: not as body,
as in planetary,
as in thing, bulk, object
but as a quickening,

a disturbance of the various
darknesses within my arms
like an eddy in the moonlit
lake where a fish moves unseen.

We rot inside, the doctor
said. To put a hand on another
is to touch death,
no doubt. Though there is also

this nebulous mist of interstellar
dust snagged by the gravity
of a few bones, mine,
but luminous:

even in the deep subarctic
of space beyond meaning, even among
the never alive, to approach
is to shine.

I hold you as I hold
water, swimming.

A STONE

On the wooden table the flame
of the lamp burns upwards without sound
and the smaller souls are called out by it
from where they have hidden during the day
in rotting stumps and the loosening
bark of trees
and hit softly against the window,
their feathery bellies licking the glass.

A loon ripples the night air
with its tune of clear silver,
the light blues,
and the one who has always been there
comes out of the shadows.

Have you had enough happiness? she says.
Have you seen
enough pain? Enough
cruelty? Have you had enough
of what there is? This
is as far as it goes.
Now are you ready for me?

Dark mother, whom I have carried with me
for years, a stone in my pocket,
I know the force of gravity
and that each thing is pulled downwards

against its will.
I will never deny you
or believe in you
only. Go back into your stone
for now. Wait for me.

SUMACS

◆

At night I leave food out
on a white plate, milk in a white cup
and sit waiting, in the kitchen chair
beside last month's newspapers
and the worn coat leaning against
the wall: the shape of you left in the air,
time seeping out of it.
In the morning nothing has been touched
again. It is the wrong time of year.

◆

Later, the days of the week unhook
from their names; the weeks unhook.
I do not lock the door
any more, but go outside and down
the bank, among the sumacs
with their tongues of dried blood
which have stopped speaking, to the pond
with its blackening water
and the one face wavering in it

wordless. Heaviness of the flesh infests me,
my skin that holds me in its nets;
I wish to change shape, as you have done
and be what you are

but that would be untrue also.

◆

I lie on the damp yellowed grass bent
as if someone has been walking here
and press my head to the ground.

Come back, I tell you.
It becomes April.

If the daffodil would shed its paper
husk and fold back into its teardrop
and then down into the earth
into its cold onion
and into sleep. The one place I can still meet you.

◆

Grief is to want more.
What use is moonlight?
I reach into it, fingers open,
and my hand is silvered
and blessed, and comes back to me holding nothing.

A BOAT

Evening comes on and the hills thicken;
red and yellow bleaching out of the leaves.
The chill pines grow their shadows.

Below them the water stills itself,
a sunset shivering in it.
One more going down to join the others.

Now the lake expands
and closes in, both.

The blackness that keeps itself
under the surface in daytime
emerges from it like mist
or as mist.

Distance vanishes, the absence
of distance pushes against the eyes.

There is no seeing the lake,
only the outlines of the hills
which are almost identical,

familiar to me as sleep,
shores unfolding upon shores
in their contours of slowed breathing.

It is touch I go by,
the boat like a hand feeling
through shoals and among
dead trees, over the boulders
lifting unseen, layer
on layer of drowned time falling away.

This is how I learned to steer
through darkness by no stars.

To be lost is only a failure of memory.

(I)

It was the pain of trees
that made this trail;
the fluid cut flesh of them only
partially hardened.
It is their scars that mark the way
we follow to the place where
the vista has closed over
and there is no more foresight.

(II)

To blaze is also to burn.
All pathways through this burning
forest open in front of you and close
behind until you lose them.

This is the forest of lost things:
abandoned boulders. Burrows.
Roots twisted into the rock.
A toad in its cool
aura; an earthstar, splayed open
and leathery, releasing dust.
None of these things knows it is lost.

(III)

We've come to a sunset, red and autumnal,
another burial. Although it is not
autumn, the wind has that chill.
Slight wind of a door closing.
The final slit of the old moon.

(IV)

I pick my way slowly
with you through the blazed forest,
scar by scar, back through
history, following the rule:

To recover what you have lost,
retrace your footsteps to the moment
at which you lost it. It will be there.

Here is the X in time.
When I am alone finally
my shadow and my own name
will come back to me.

(V)

I kneel and dig with my knifeblade
in the soil and find nothing.
I have forgotten what I hid here.

It must be the body of clear air
I left here carefully buried
and thought I could always
come back to and inhabit.

I thought I could be with myself only.
I thought I could float.
I thought I would always have a choice.
Now I am earthbound.
An incarnation.

(VI)

This is the last walk
I will take with you in your absence.

Your skin flares where I touch it,
then fades and the wood solidifies
around you. We are this momentary.

How much I love you.
I would like to be wise and calm.

I would make you eternal,
I would hold back your death if I could,
but where would you be without it?

We can live forever,
but only from time to time.

(VII)

Now we have reached the rocky point
and the shore, and the sky is deepening,
though the water still holds light
and gives it out, like fumes
or like fire. I wait, listening to that
place where a sound should be
and is not,
which is not my heart
or yours, which is darker
and more solitary,
which approaches. Which is the sound
the earth will make for itself
without us. A stone echoing a stone.
The pines rushing motionless.

Darkness waits apart from any occasion for it;
like sorrow it is always available.
This is only one kind,

the kind in which there are stars
above the leaves, brilliant as steel nails
and countless and without regard.

We are walking together
on dead wet leaves in the intermoon
among the looming nocturnal rocks
which would be pinkish grey
in daylight, gnawed and softened
by moss and ferns, which would be green,
in the musty fresh yeast smell
of trees rotting, earth returning
itself to itself

and I take your hand, which is the shape a hand
would be if you existed truly.
I wish to show you the darkness
you are so afraid of.

Trust me. This darkness
is a place you can enter and be
as safe in as you are anywhere;
you can put one foot in front of the other
and believe the sides of your eyes.
Memorize it. You will know it
again in your own time.
When the appearances of things have left you,
you will still have this darkness.
Something of your own you can carry with you.

We have come to the edge:
the lake gives off its hush;
in the outer night there is a barred owl
calling, like a moth
against the ear, from the far shore
which is invisible.
The lake, vast and dimensionless,
doubles everything, the stars,
the boulders, itself, even the darkness
that you can walk so long in
it becomes light.

FROM

SELECTED

POEMS II

✦ ✦ ✦

The front lawn is littered with young men
who want me to pay attention to them
not to their bodies and their freshly
washed cotton skins, not to their enticing
motifs of bulb and root, but
to their poems. In the back yard
on the other hand are the older men
who want me to pay attention to their
bodies. Ah men,
why do you want
all this attention?
I can write poems for myself, make
love to a doorknob if absolutely
necessary. What do you have to offer me
I can't find otherwise
except humiliation? Which I no longer
need. I gather
dust, for practice, my attention
wanders like a household pet
once leashed, now
out on the prowl, an animal
neither dog nor cat, unique
and hairy, snuffling
among the damp leaves at the foot
of the hedge, among the afterbloom
of irises which melt like blue and purple
ice back into air; hunting for something
lost, something to eat or love, among
the twists of earth,
among the glorious bearclaw sun-
sets, evidence
of the red life that is leaking
out of me into time, which become
each night more final.

I used to have tricks, dodges, a whole sackful.
I could outfox anyone,
double back, cover my tracks,
walk backwards, the works.
I left it somewhere, that knack
of running, that good luck.

Now I have only
one trick left: head down, spikes out,
brain tucked in.
I can roll up:
thistle as animal, a flower of quills,
that's about it.

I lie in the grass and watch the sunlight pleating
the skin on the backs of my hands
as if I were a toad, squashed and drying.

I don't even wade through spring water
to cover my scent.
I can't be bothered.

I squat and stink, thinking:
peace and quiet are worth something.
Here I am, dogs,
nose me over,
go away sneezing, snouts full of barbs
hooking their way to your brain.
Now you've got some
of my pain. Much good may it do you.

I prop up my face and go out, avoiding the sunlight,
keeping away from the curve where the burnt road
touches the sky.
Whatever exists at the earth's centre will get me
sooner or later. Sooner. Than I think.
That core of light squeezed tight
and shut, dense as a star, as molten
mirrors. Dark red and heavy. Slab at the butcher's.
Already it's dragging me down, already
I become shorter, infinitesimally.
The bones of my legs thicken—that's first—
contract, like muscles.
After that comes the frailty, a dry wind blowing
inside my body,
scouring me from within, as if I were
a fossil, the soft parts eaten away.
Soon I will turn to calcium. It starts with the heart.

I do a lot of washing. I wash everything.
If I could only get this clean once, before I die.

To see God, they told me, you do not go
into the forest or city; not the meadow,
the seashore even unless it is cold.
You go to the desert.
You think of sand.

Nightshade grows more densely than most weeds:
in the country of burdock and random stones,
rooted in undersides of damp logs,
leaf mould, worm castings.
Dark foliage, strong tendrils, the flowers purple
for mourning but with a centre
so yellow I thought *buttercup* or *adder,*
the berries red, translucent,
like the eggs of an unknown moth,
feather-soft, nocturnal.
Belladonna was its name, *beautiful lady.*
Its other name was *deadly.*
If you ate it, it would stop your heart,
you would sleep forever. I was told that.
Sometimes it was used for healing,
or in the eyes. I learned that later.

I had to go down the mud path to the ravine,
the wooden bridge across it rotting,
walk across it, from good
board to good board,
level with the tips of the trees.
Birds I don't remember.
On the other side the thicket of nightshade
where cats hunted, leaving their piss:
a smell of ammonia and rust, some dead thing.
All this in sunshine.

At that time I did well, my fingers
were eaten down to the blood.
They never healed.
The word *nightshade* a shadow,
the colour of a recurring dream
in which you cannot see colour.
Porridge, worn underwear, wool

stockings, my fault. Not purple: some
other colour. Sick
outside in a snowbank.

I dreamed of falling from the bridge,
one hand holding on, unable to call.
In other dreams, I could step into the air.
It was not flying. I never flew.

Now some years I cross the new bridge,
concrete, the path white gravel.
The old bridge is gone,
the nightshade has been cut down.
The nightshade spreads and thickens
where it always was,
at this season the red berries.
You would be tempted to eat them
if you did not know better.
Also the purple flowers.

MOTHERS

How much havoc this woman spills
out of herself into us
merely by being
unhappy with such finality:

The mothers rise up in us,
rustling, uttering cooing
sounds, their hands moving
into our hands, patting anything
smooth again. Her deprived eyes and deathcamp
shoulders. There there

we say, bringing
bright things in desperation:
a flower? We make
dolls of other people and offer
them to her. Have him, we say,
what about her? Eat their heads off
for all we care, but stop crying.

She half sits in the bed, shaking
her head under the cowl of hair.
Nothing will do, ever.

She discards us, crumples down
into the sheets, twisting around
that space we can never
hope to fill,
hugging her true mother,
the one who left her here
not among us:
hugging her darkness.

SHE

The snake hunts and sinews
his way along and is not his own
idea of viciousness. All he wants is
a fast grab, with fur and a rapid
pulse, so he can take that fluttering
and make it him, do a transfusion.
They say *whip* or *rope* about him, but this
does not give the idea; nor
phallus, which has no bones,
kills nothing and cannot see.
The snake sees red, like a hand held
above sunburn. Zeroes in,
which means, aims for the round egg
with nothing in it but blood.
If lucky, misses the blade
slicing light just behind him.
He's our idea of a bad time, we are his.
I say *he* out of habit. It could be *she*.

Whether it is possible to become lost.

Whether one tree looks like another.
Whether there is water all around
the edges or not. Whether
there are edges or whether
there are just insects.

Whether the insects bite,
whether you would die
from the bites of the insects.
Whether you would die.

Whether you would die for your country.
Whether anyone in the country would die for your country.
Let's be honest here.
A layer of snow, a layer of granite, a layer of snow.
What you think lies under the snow.
What you think lies.

Whether you think white on white is a state of mind
or blue on blue or green on green.
Whether you think there is a state,
of mind.

How many clothes you have to take off
before you can make love.
This I think is important:
the undoing of buttons, the gradual shedding
of one colour after another. It leads
to the belief that what you see is not
what you get.

Whether there are preliminaries,
hallways, vestibules,

basements, furnaces,
chesterfields, silences
between sentences, between pieces
of furniture, parasites in your eyes,
drinkable water.

Whether there has ever been
an invading army.
Whether, if there were an invading army,
you would collaborate.
Poor boy, you'd say, he looks cold
standing out there, and he's only twenty.
From his point of view this must be hell.

A fur coat is what he needs,
a cup of tea, a cup of coffee,
a warm body.
Whether on the contrary
you'd slit his throat in his sleep
or in yours. I ask you.

So, you are a nice person.
You would behave well.
What you mean by behaving well.
When the outline of a man
whose face you cannot see
appears at your bedroom window,
whether you would shoot.
If you had a gun, that is.
Whether you would have a gun.

MACHINE. GUN. NEST.

The blood goes through your neck veins with a noise they call
   singing.
Time shatters like bad glass; you are this pinpoint of it.

Your feet rotting inside your boots, the skin of your chest
festering under the zippers, the waterproof armour,

you sit here, on the hill, a vantage point, at this X or scuffling
in the earth, which they call a nest. Who chose that word?

Whatever you are you are not an egg, or a bird either.
Vipers perhaps is what was meant. Who cares now?

That is the main question: who cares. Not these pieces of paper
from somewhere known as *home* you fold, unread, in your pocket.

Each landscape is a state of mind, he once told me:
mountains for awe and remoteness, meadows for calm and the
   steam

of the lulled senses. But some views are slippery.
This place is both beautiful as the sun and full of menace:

dark green, with now and then a red splotch, like a punctured
vein, white like a flare; stench of the half-eaten.
Look at it carefully, see what it hides, or it will burst in your head.

If you lose your nerve you may die, if you don't lose it
you may die anyway, the joke goes. What is your nerve?

It is turning the world flat, the moon to a disc you could aim at,
popping the birds off the fence wire. Delight in accuracy,

no attention paid to results, dead singing, the smear of feathers.
You know you were more than that, but best to forget it.

There's no slack time for memory here; when you can, you plunge
into some inert woman as into a warm bath; for a moment
comforting, and of no consequence, like sucking your thumb.

No woman can imagine this. What you do to them
is therefore incidental, and also your just reward,

though sometimes, in a gap in the action, there's a space
for the concepts of *sister, mother*. Like folded laundry. They come
    and go.

But stick your hand up a woman, alive or freshly
dead, it is much like a gutted chicken:
giblets, a body cavity. Killing can be

merely a kind of impatience, at the refusal
of this to mean anything to you. He told me that.

You wanted to go in sharp and clean with a sword,
do what they once called battle. Now you just want your life.

There's not much limit to what you would do to get it.
Justice and *mercy* are words that happen in cool rooms, elsewhere.

Are you your brother's keeper? Yes or no, depending
what clothes he has on, what hair. There is more than one brother.

What you need to contend with now is the hard Easter-
eggshell blue of the sky, that shows you too clearly

the mass of deep green trees leaning slowly towards you
as if on the verge of speech, or annunciation.

More likely some break in the fabric of sight, or a sad mistake
you will hear about in the moment you make it. Some glint of
 reflected light.

That whir in the space where your left hand was is not singing.
Death is the bird that hatches, is fed, comes flying.

The rest of us watch from beyond the fence
as the woman moves with her jagged stride
into her pain as if into a slow race.
We see her body in motion
but hear no sounds, or we hear
sounds but no language; or we know
it is not a language we know
yet. We can see her clearly
but for her it is running in black smoke.
The clusters of cells in her swelling
like porridge boiling, and bursting,
like grapes, we think. Or we think of
explosions in mud; but we know nothing.
All around us the trees
and the grasses light up with forgiveness,
so green and at this time
of the year healthy.
We would like to call something
out to her. Some form of cheering.
There is pain but no arrival at anything.

Strawberries, pears, fingers, the eyes
of snails: the other shapes water
takes. Even leaves are liquid
arrested. To die
is to dry, lose juice,
the sweet pulp sucked out. To enter
the time of rind and stone.

Your clothes hang shrivelling
in the closet, your other body once
filled with your breath.
When I say *body,* what
is that a word for?
Why should the word *you*
remain attached to that suffering?
Wave upon wave, as we say.

I think of your hair burning
first, a scant minute
of halo; later, an afterglow
of bone, red slash of sunset.
The body a cinder or luminescent
saint, or Turner seascape.

Fine words, but why do I want
to tart up death?
Which needs no decoration,
which is only a boat,
plain and wooden
and ordinary, without eyes
painted on it,
sightless and hidden
in fog and going somewhere
else. Away from the shore.

My dear, my voyager, my scant handful
of ashes: I'd scatter you
if I could, this way, on the river.
A wave is neither form
nor energy. Both. Neither.

I

The arbutus trees, with their bark like burned skin
that has healed, enclosing someone's real arms
in the moment of reaching, but not towards you:

you know they are paying no attention
to you and your failed love and equivocation.

Why do you wish to be forgiven by them?

Yet you are, and you breathe in,
and the new moon sheds grace without intention.

II

You lie on your stomach
looking down through a crack between rocks:

the seaweed with its bladders and hairs,
the genital bodies hinted
by the pink flanges of limpets,
five starfish, each thickened purple arm
a drowning tongue,
the sea's membrane, with its wet shine
and pulse, and no promise.

There is no future,
really there is none
and no salvation

To know this is salvation

III

Where the rock stops upland, thistles burning
at the tips, leaving their white ash

A result of the sun, this pentecost
and conflagration.

Light flares up off the tidepool
where the barnacles grasp at the water
each with its one skeletal hand
which is also a frond

which is also a tongue
which is also a flame
you are praised by

IV

Sandrock the colour of erosion,
pushed by the wind
into gills and clefts
and heavy folds like snow melting
or the crease of a doubled arm

There ought to be caves here

The sunlight
slides over the body like pollen

A door is about to open
onto paradise. Onto a beach like this one,

exactly like it, down to each thistle,
down to the red halfcrab eaten on the sand,
down to the rubber glove
gone white and blinded,
wedged in and stranded by the tide

down to the loss because you
can never truly be here.

Can this be paradise, with so much loss
in it?

     Paradise
is defined by loss.
               Is loss.
Is.

Went up the steep stone hill, thinking,
My trick hip could fail me. Went up anyway
to see the flower with three names:
chocolate lilies, for the colour,
stink lilies for the smell, red meat going off,
squaw lilies. Thought what I would be like, falling.
Brain spilled on the rocks.
Said to her: never seen these before. Why squaw?
Oh, she said, something to do
with the smell.
When she said that I felt as if painted
naked on an off-blue sofa
by a bad expressionist, ochre
and dirty greens, lips thickened with yellow
pigment, a red-infected
crevice dividing the splayed legs.
Thought: this is what it is, to be part
of the landscape. Subject to
depiction. Thought:
release the lilies. They have nothing
to do with these names for them.
Not even lilies.
Went down the steep stone hill. Did not fall.

◆

The dipper, small dust-coloured bird with robin
feet, walks on the stream bed
enclosed in its nimbus of silver
air, miraculous bubble, a non-miracle.
Who could have thought it? We think it now,
and liverwort on a dead log, earthstar,
hand, finger by finger.

◆

For you, at last, I'd like to make
something uncomplicated; some neither god
nor goddess, not between, beyond
them; pinch it from dough,
bake it in the oven, a stone in its belly.
Stones lined up on the windowsill,
picked off some beach or other for being holy.

◆

The hookworm, in the eye of
the universe, which is the unsteady gaze
of eternity maybe, is beloved. How could it not be,
living so blessed, in its ordained red meadows
of blood where it waves like a seaweed?
Praise be, it sings with its dracula mouth.
Praise be.

◆ ◆ ◆

What idiocy could transform the moon, that old sea-overgrown
skull seen from above, to a goddess of mercy?

You fish for the silver light, there on the quiet lake, so clear
to see; you plunge your hands into the water and come up empty.

Don't ask questions of stones. They will rightly ignore you,
they have shoulders but no mouths, their conversation is elsewhere.

Expect nothing else from the perfect white birdbones, picked clean
in the sedge in the cup of muskeg: you are none of their business.

Fresh milk in a glass on a plastic tray, a choice of breakfast
foods; we sit at the table, discussing the theories of tragedy.

The plump pink-faced men in the metal chairs at the edge of the
    golf course
adding things up, sunning themselves, adding things up.

The corpse, washed and dressed, beloved meat pumped full of
    chemicals
and burned, if turned back into money could feed two hundred.

Voluptuousness of the newspaper; scratching your back on the
    bad news;
furious anger in spring sunshine, a plate of fruit on the table.

Ask of the apple, crisp heart, ask the pear or suave banana
which necks got sucked, whose flesh got stewed, so we could
    love them.

The slug, a muscular jelly, slippery and luminous, dirty
eggwhite unrolling its ribbon of mucus—this too is delicious.

The oily slick, rainbow-coloured, spread on the sewage
flats in the back field is beautiful also

as is the man's hand cut off at the wrist and nailed to a treetrunk,
mute and imploring, as if asking for alms, or held up in warning.

Who knows what it tells you? It does not say, beg, *Have mercy,*
it is too late for that. Perhaps only, *I too was here once, where you are.*

The star-like flower by the path, by the ferns, in the rain-
forest, whose name I did not know, and the war in the jungle—

the war in the jungle, blood on the crushed ferns, whose name I
    do not
know, and the star-like flower grow out of the same earth

whose name I do not know. Whose name for itself I do not know.
Or much else, except that the moon is no goddess of mercy

but shines on us each damp warm night of her full rising
as if she were, and that is why we keep asking

the wrong questions, he said, of the wrong things. The questions
    of things.
                                        Ask the spider
what is the name of God, she will tell you: God is a spider.

Let the other moons pray to the moon. Oh Goddess of Mercy,
you who are not the moon, or anything we can see clearly,

we need to know each other's names and what we are asking.
Do not be any thing. Be the light we see by.

MORNING

IN THE

BURNED HOUSE

❖ ❖ ❖

You come back into the room
where you've been living
all along. You say:
What's been going on
while I was away? Who
got those sheets dirty, and why
are there no more grapefruit?
Setting foot on the middle ground
between body and word, which contains,
or is supposed to, other
people. You know it was you
who slept, who ate here, though you don't
believe it. I must have taken
time off, you think, for the buttered
toast and the love and maybe both
at once, which would account for the
grease on the bedspread, but no,
now you're certain, someone else
has been here wearing
your clothes and saying
words for you, because there was no time off.

You're sad because you're sad.
It's psychic. It's the age. It's chemical.
Go see a shrink or take a pill,
or hug your sadness like an eyeless doll
you need to sleep.

Well, all children are sad
but some get over it.
Count your blessings. Better than that,
buy a hat. Buy a coat or pet.
Take up dancing to forget.

Forget what?
Your sadness, your shadow,
whatever it was that was done to you
the day of the lawn party
when you came inside flushed with the sun,
your mouth sulky with sugar,
in your new dress with the ribbon
and the ice-cream smear,
and said to yourself in the bathroom,
I am not the favourite child.

My darling, when it comes
right down to it
and the light fails and the fog rolls in
and you're trapped in your overturned body
under a blanket or burning car,

and the red flame is seeping out of you
and igniting the tarmac beside your head
or else the floor, or else the pillow,
none of us is;
or else we all are.

In the secular night you wander around
alone in your house. It's two-thirty.
Everyone has deserted you,
or this is your story;
you remember it from being sixteen,
when the others were out somewhere, having a good time,
or so you suspected,
and you had to babysit.
You took a large scoop of vanilla ice cream
and filled up the glass with grapejuice
and ginger ale, and put on Glenn Miller
with his big-band sound,
and lit a cigarette and blew the smoke up the chimney,
and cried for a while because you were not dancing,
and then danced, by yourself, your mouth circled with purple.

Now, forty years later, things have changed,
and it's baby lima beans.
It's necessary to reserve a secret vice.
This is what comes from forgetting to eat
at the stated mealtimes. You simmer them carefully,
drain, add cream and pepper,
and amble up and down the stairs,
scooping them up with your fingers right out of the bowl,
talking to yourself out loud.
You'd be surprised if you got an answer,
but that part will come later.

There is so much silence between the words,
you say. You say, The sensed absence
of God and the sensed presence
amount to much the same thing,
only in reverse.
You say, I have too much white clothing.
You start to hum.

Several hundred years ago
this could have been mysticism
or heresy. It isn't now.
Outside there are sirens.
Someone's been run over.
The century grinds on.

RED FOX

The red fox crosses the ice
intent on none of my business.
It's winter and slim pickings.

I stand in the bushy cemetery,
pretending to watch birds,
but really watching the fox
who could care less.
She pauses on the sheer glare
of the pond. She knows I'm there,
sniffs me in the wind at her shoulder.
If I had a gun or dog
or a raw heart, she'd smell it.
She didn't get this smart for nothing.

She's a lean vixen: I can see
the ribs, the sly
trickster's eyes, filled with longing
and desperation, the skinny
feet, adept at lies.

Why encourage the notion
of virtuous poverty?

It's only an excuse
for zero charity.
Hunger corrupts, and absolute hunger
corrupts absolutely,
or almost. Of course there are mothers,
squeezing their breasts
dry, pawning their bodies,
shedding teeth for their children,
or that's our fond belief.
But remember—Hansel
and Gretel were dumped in the forest

because their parents were starving.
Sauve qui peut. To survive
we'd all turn thief

and rascal, or so says the fox,
with her coat of an elegant scoundrel,
her white knife of a smile,
who knows just where she's going:

to steal something
that doesn't belong to her—
some chicken, or one more chance,
or other life.

How much longer can I get away
with being so fucking cute?
Not much longer.
The shoes with bows, the cunning underwear
with slogans on the crotch—*Knock Here,*
and so forth—
will have to go, along with the cat suit.
After a while you forget
what you really look like.
You think your mouth is the size it was.
You pretend not to care.

When I was young I went with my hair
hiding one eye, thinking myself daring;
off to the movies in my jaunty pencil
skirt and elastic cinch-belt,
chewed gum, left lipstick
imprints the shape of grateful, rubbery
sighs on the cigarettes of men
I hardly knew and didn't want to.
Men were a skill, you had to have
good hands, breathe into
their nostrils, as for horses. It was something I did well,
like playing the flute, although I don't.

In the forests of grey stems there are standing pools,
tarn-coloured, choked with brown leaves.
Through them you can see an arm, a shoulder,
when the light is right, with the sky clouded.
The train goes past silos, through meadows,
the winter wheat on the fields like scanty fur.

I still get letters, although not many.
A man writes me, requesting true-life stories
about bad sex. He's doing an anthology.

He got my name off an old calendar,
the photo that's mostly bum and daisies,
back when my skin had the golden slick
of fresh-spread margarine.
Not rape, he says, but disappointment,
more like a defeat of expectations.
Dear Sir, I reply, I never had any.
Bad sex, that is.
It was never the sex, it was the other things,
the absence of flowers, the death threats,
the eating habits at breakfast.
I notice I'm using the past tense.

Though the vaporous cloud of chemicals that enveloped you
like a glowing eggshell, an incense,
doesn't disappear: it just gets larger
and takes in more. You grow out
of sex like a shrunk dress
into your common senses, those you share
with whatever's listening. The way the sun
moves through the hours becomes important,
the smeared raindrops
on the window, buds
on the roadside weeds, the sheen
of spilled oil in a raw ditch
filling with muddy water.

Don't get me wrong: with the lights out
I'd still take on anyone,
if I had the energy to spare.
But after a while these flesh arpeggios get boring,
like Bach over and over;
too much of one kind of glory.

When I was all body I was lazy.
I had an easy life, and was not grateful.
Now there are more of me.
Don't confuse me with my hen-leg elbows:
what you get is no longer
what you see.

She reclines, more or less.
Try that posture, it's hardly languor.
Her right arm sharp angles.
With her left she conceals her ambush.
Shoes but not stockings,
how sinister. The flower
behind her ear is naturally
not real, of a piece
with the sofa's drapery.
The windows (if any) are shut.
This is indoor sin.
Above the head of the (clothed) maid
is an invisible voice balloon: *Slut*.

But. Consider the body,
unfragile, defiant, the pale nipples
staring you right in the bull's-eye.
Consider also the black ribbon
around the neck. What's under it?
A fine red threadline, where the head
was taken off and glued back on.
The body's on offer,
but the neck's as far as it goes.

This is no morsel.
Put clothes on her and you'd have a schoolteacher,
the kind with the brittle whiphand.

There's someone else in this room.
You, Monsieur Voyeur.
As for that object of yours
she's seen those before, and better.

I, the head, am the only subject
of this picture.
You, Sir, are furniture.
Get stuffed.

Somehow I never succeeded
in being taken seriously. They made me
wear things that were ruffled: off-the-
shoulder blouses, the tiered skirts
of flouncing Spanish dancers, though I never
quite got the hauteur—I was always tempted
to wink, show instead of a tragic
outstretched neck, a slice of flank. Now look
at me: a vaginal hot pink,
vibrant as a laxative bottle—
not, given the company, a respectable
colour. Let's face it: when I was in
the flesh, to be beautiful and to be
a woman was a kind
of joke. The men wanted to nail
me in the trophy room, on the pool-
table if possible, the women simply to poke
my eyes out. Me, I would have preferred
to enjoy myself—a little careless
love, some laughs, a few drinks
but that was not an option.

What would have given
me weight? Substance? For them.
Long canines? Vengeance?
A stiletto hidden in my skirt,
a greyish rainbow of fate
like an aureole of rancid lard—
or better: dress up in armour,
ride across the steppes, leading a horde
of armed murderers. That gets you a statue,
copper or stone, with a lofty frown
—jaw clenched as if chewing—

like those erected by the sober
citizens, years later,
for all the sad destroyers.

Well, to hell with them. I'd rather
be a flower, even this one, so much like
a toilet-paper decoration
at a high-school dance.
Even that, to be trampled
underfoot next day by the janitor
sweeping up, even the damp flirtation,
the crumpled tulle, even the botched smooch
in the parking lot, the boy with the fat neck
and the hip flask, even the awkward fumbling
with the wired bodice, cheap perfume between
the freckled breasts, would have been better
than all their history, the smudged
flags, dry parchments, layers of dead bone
they find so solemn, the slaughters
they like to memorize, and tell
their children also to pray to

here, where they hate bouquets, the pleasures
of thoughtless botany, a glass
of wine or two on the terrace,
bare leg against white trouser
under the table, that ancient ploy
and vital puzzle, water-
of-life cliche that keeps things going,
tawdry and priceless, the breeze
that riffles through what now
may be my leaves, my green closed
eyes, my negligible
vulgar fragile incandescent petals,
these many mouths, lipsticked and showy
and humid as kisses opening
in a hothouse, oh I'd give anything

to have it back again, in
the flesh, the flesh,
which was all the time
I ever had for anything. The joy.

The world is full of women
who'd tell me I should be ashamed of myself
if they had the chance. Quit dancing.
Get some self-respect
and a day job.
Right. And minimum wage,
and varicose veins, just standing
in one place for eight hours
behind a glass counter
bundled up to the neck, instead of
naked as a meat sandwich.
Selling gloves, or something.
Instead of what I do sell.
You have to have talent
to peddle a thing so nebulous
and without material form.
Exploited, they'd say. Yes, any way
you cut it, but I've a choice
of how, and I'll take the money.

I do give value.
Like preachers, I sell vision,
like perfume ads, desire
or its facsimile. Like jokes
or war, it's all in the timing.
I sell men back their worst suspicions:
that everything's for sale,
and piecemeal. They gaze at me and see
a chain-saw murder just before it happens,
when thigh, ass, inkblot, crevice, tit, and nipple
are still connected.
Such hatred leaps in them,
my beery worshippers! That, or a bleary
hopeless love. Seeing the rows of heads
and upturned eyes, imploring

but ready to snap at my ankles,
I understand floods and earthquakes, and the urge
to step on ants. I keep the beat,
and dance for them because
they can't. The music smells like foxes,
crisp as heated metal
searing the nostrils
or humid as August, hazy and languorous
as a looted city the day after,
when all the rape's been done
already, and the killing,
and the survivors wander around
looking for garbage
to eat, and there's only a bleak exhaustion.

Speaking of which, it's the smiling
tires me out the most.
This, and the pretence
that I can't hear them.
And I can't, because I'm after all
a foreigner to them.
The speech here is all warty gutturals,
obvious as a slab of ham,
but I come from the province of the gods
where meanings are lilting and oblique.
I don't let on to everyone,
but lean close, and I'll whisper:
My mother was raped by a holy swan.
You believe that? You can take me out to dinner.
That's what we tell all the husbands.
There sure are a lot of dangerous birds around.

Not that anyone here
but you would understand.
The rest of them would like to watch me
and feel nothing. Reduce me to components
as in a clock factory or abattoir.
Crush out the mystery.

Wall me up alive
in my own body.
They'd like to see through me,
but nothing is more opaque
than absolute transparency.
Look—my feet don't hit the marble!
Like breath or a balloon, I'm rising,
I hover six inches in the air
in my blazing swan-egg of light.
You think I'm not a goddess?
Try me.
This is a torch song.
Touch me and you'll burn.

Men and their mournful romanticisms
that can't get the dishes done—
that's freedom, that broken wineglass
in the cold fireplace.

When women wash underpants, it's a chore.
When men do it, an intriguing affliction.
How plangent, the damp socks flapping on the line,
how lost and single in the orphaning air . . .

She cherishes that sadness,
tells him to lie down on the grass,
closes each of his eyes with a finger,
applies her body like a poultice.

You poor thing, said the Australian woman
while he held our baby—
as if I had forced him to do it,
as if I had my high heel in his face.

Still, who's taken in?
Every time?
Us, and our empty hands, the hands
of starving nurses.

It's bullet holes we want to see in their skin,
scars, and the chance to touch them.

CELL

Now look objectively. You have to
admit the cancer cell is beautiful.
If it were a flower, you'd say, *How pretty,*
with its mauve centre and pink petals

or if a cover for a pulpy thirties
sci-fi magazine, *How striking;*
as an alien, a success,
all purple eye and jelly tentacles
and spines, or are they gills,
creeping around on granular Martian
dirt red as the inside of the body,

while its tender walls
expand and burst, its spores
scatter elsewhere, take root, like money,
drifting like a fiction or
miasma in and out of people's
brains, digging themselves
industriously in. The lab technician

says, *It has forgotten
how to die.* But why remember? All it wants is more
amnesia. More life, and more abundantly. To take
more. To eat more. To replicate itself. To keep on
doing those things forever. Such desires
are not unknown. Look in the mirror.

Confess: it's my profession
that alarms you.
This is why few people ask me to dinner,
though Lord knows I don't go out of my way to be scary.
I wear dresses of sensible cut
and unalarming shades of beige,
I smell of lavender and go to the hairdresser's:
no prophetess mane of mine,
complete with snakes, will frighten the youngsters.
If I roll my eyes and mutter,
if I clutch at my heart and scream in horror
like a third-rate actress chewing up a mad scene,
I do it in private and nobody sees
but the bathroom mirror.

In general I might agree with you:
women should not contemplate war,
should not weigh tactics impartially,
or evade the word *enemy,*
or view both sides and denounce nothing.
Women should march for peace,
or hand out white feathers to arouse bravery,
spit themselves on bayonets
to protect their babies,
whose skulls will be split anyway,
or, having been raped repeatedly,
hang themselves with their own hair.
These are the functions that inspire general comfort.
That, and the knitting of socks for the troops
and a sort of moral cheerleading.
Also: mourning the dead.
Sons, lovers, and so forth.
All the killed children.

Instead of this, I tell
what I hope will pass as truth.
A blunt thing, not lovely.
The truth is seldom welcome,
especially at dinner,
though I am good at what I do.
My trade is courage and atrocities.
I look at them and do not condemn.
I write things down the way they happened,
as near as can be remembered.
I don't ask *why,* because it is mostly the same.
Wars happen because the ones who start them
think they can win.

In my dreams there is glamour.
The Vikings leave their fields
each year for a few months of killing and plunder,
much as the boys go hunting.
In real life they were farmers.
They come back loaded with splendour.
The Arabs ride against Crusaders
with scimitars that could sever
silk in the air.
A swift cut to the horse's neck
and a hunk of armour crashes down
like a tower. Fire against metal.
A poet might say: romance against banality.
When awake, I know better.

Despite the propaganda, there are no monsters,
or none that can be finally buried.
Finish one off, and circumstances
and the radio create another.
Believe me: whole armies have prayed fervently
to God all night and meant it,
and been slaughtered anyway.
Brutality wins frequently,
and large outcomes have turned on the invention

of a mechanical device, viz. radar.
True, valour sometimes counts for something,
as at Thermopylae. Sometimes being right—
though ultimate virtue, by agreed tradition,
is decided by the winner.
Sometimes men throw themselves on grenades
and burst like paper bags of guts
to save their comrades.
I can admire that.
But rats and cholera have won many wars.
Those, and potatoes,
or the absence of them.
It's no use pinning all those medals
across the chests of the dead.
Impressive, but I know too much.
Grand exploits merely depress me.

In the interests of research
I have walked on many battlefields
that once were liquid with pulped
men's bodies and spangled with exploded
shells and splayed bone.
All of them have been green again
by the time I got there.
Each has inspired a few good quotes in its day.
Sad marble angels brood like hens
over the grassy nests where nothing hatches.
(The angels could just as well be described as *vulgar*
or *pitiless,* depending on camera angle.)
The word *glory* figures a lot on gateways.
Of course I pick a flower or two
from each, and press it in the hotel Bible
for a souvenir.
I'm just as human as you.

But it's no use asking me for a final statement.
As I say, I deal in tactics.
Also statistics:
for every year of peace there have been four hundred
years of war.

"Half-Hanged Mary" was Mary Webster, who was accused of
witchcraft in the 1680s in a Puritan town in Massachusetts and hanged
from a tree—where, according to one of the several surviving accounts,
she was left all night. It is known that when she was cut down she was
still alive, since she lived for another fourteen years.

7 P.M.

Rumour was loose in the air,
hunting for some neck to land on.
I was milking the cow,
the barn door open to the sunset.

I didn't feel the aimed word hit
and go in like a soft bullet.
I didn't feel the smashed flesh
closing over it like water
over a thrown stone.

I was hanged for living alone,
for having blue eyes and a sunburned skin,
tattered skirts, few buttons,
a weedy farm in my own name,
and a surefire cure for warts;

Oh yes, and breasts,
and a sweet pear hidden in my body.
Whenever there's talk of demons
these come in handy.

8 P.M.

The rope was an improvisation.
With time they'd have thought of axes.

Up I go like a windfall in reverse,
a blackened apple stuck back onto the tree.

Trussed hands, rag in my mouth,
a flag raised to salute the moon,

old bone-faced goddess, old original,
who once took blood in return for food.

The men of the town stalk homeward,
excited by their show of hate,

their own evil turned inside out like a glove,
and me wearing it.

    9 P.M.

The bonnets come to stare,
the dark skirts also,
the upturned faces in between,
mouths closed so tight they're lipless.
I can see down into their eyeholes
and nostrils. I can see their fear.

You were my friend, you too.
I cured your baby, Mrs.,
and flushed yours out of you,
Non-wife, to save your life.

Help me down? You don't dare.
I might rub off on you,
like soot or gossip. Birds
of a feather burn together,
though as a rule ravens are singular.

In a gathering like this one
the safe place is the background,

pretending you can't dance,
the safe stance pointing a finger.

I understand. You can't spare
anything, a hand, a piece of bread, a shawl
against the cold,
a good word. Lord
knows there isn't much
to go around. You need it all.

10 P.M.

Well, God, now that I'm up here
with maybe some time to kill
away from the daily
fingerwork, legwork, work
at the hen level,
we can continue our quarrel,
the one about free will.

Is it my choice that I'm dangling
like a turkey's wattles from this
more than indifferent tree?
If Nature is Your alphabet,
what letter is this rope?

Does my twisting body spell out Grace?
I hurt, therefore I am.
Faith, Charity, and Hope
are three dead angels
falling like meteors or
burning owls across
the profound blank sky of Your face.

12 MIDNIGHT

My throat is taut against the rope
choking off words and air;

I'm reduced to knotted muscle.
Blood bulges in my skull,
my clenched teeth hold it in;
I bite down on despair.

Death sits on my shoulder like a crow
waiting for my squeezed beet
of a heart to burst
so he can eat my eyes

or like a judge
muttering about sluts and punishment
and licking his lips

or like a dark angel
insidious in his glossy feathers
whispering to me to be easy
on myself. To breathe out finally.
Trust me, he says, caressing
me. *Why suffer?*

A temptation, to sink down
into these definitions.
To become a martyr in reverse,
or food, or trash.

To give up my own words for myself,
my own refusals.
To give up knowing.
To give up pain.
To let go.

2 A.M.

Out of my mouth is coming, at some
distance from me, a thin gnawing sound
which you could confuse with prayer except that
praying is not constrained.

Or is it, Lord?
Maybe it's more like being strangled
than I once thought. Maybe it's
a gasp for air, prayer.
Did those men at Pentecost
want flames to shoot out of their heads?
Did they ask to be tossed
on the ground, gabbling like holy poultry,
eyeballs bulging?

As mine are, as mine are.
There is only one prayer; it is not
the knees in the clean nightgown
on the hooked rug,
I want this, I want that.
Oh far beyond.
Call it *Please.* Call it *Mercy.*
Call it *Not yet, not yet,*
as Heaven threatens to explode
inwards in fire and shredded flesh, and the angels caw.

3 A.M.

wind seethes in the leaves around
me the trees exude night
birds night birds yell inside
my ears like stabbed hearts my heart
stutters in my fluttering cloth
body I dangle with strength
going out of me the wind seethes
in my body tattering
the words I clench
my fists hold No
talisman or silver disc my lungs
flail as if drowning I call
on you as witness I did
no crime I was born I have borne I
bear I will be born this is

a crime I will not
acknowledge leaves and wind
hold on to me
I will not give in

6 A.M.

Sun comes up, huge and blaring,
no longer a simile for God.
Wrong address. I've been out there.

Time is relative, let me tell you
I have lived a millennium.

I would like to say my hair turned white
overnight, but it didn't.
Instead it was my heart:
bleached out like meat in water.

Also, I'm about three inches taller.
This is what happens when you drift in space
listening to the gospel
of the red-hot stars.
Pinpoints of infinity riddle my brain,
a revelation of deafness.

At the end of my rope
I testify to silence.
Don't say I'm not grateful.

Most will have only one death.
I will have two.

8 A.M.

When they came to harvest my corpse
(open your mouth, close your eyes)
cut my body from the rope,

surprise, surprise:
I was still alive.

Tough luck, folks,
I know the law:
you can't execute me twice
for the same thing. How nice.

I fell to the clover, breathed it in,
and bared my teeth at them
in a filthy grin.
You can imagine how that went over.

Now I only need to look
out at them through my sky-blue eyes.
They see their own ill will
staring them in the forehead
and turn tail.

Before, I was not a witch.
But now I am one.

LATER

My body of skin waxes and wanes
around my true body,
a tender nimbus.
I skitter over the paths and fields
mumbling to myself like crazy,
mouth full of juicy adjectives
and purple berries.
The townsfolk dive headfirst into the bushes
to get out of my way.

My first death orbits my head,
an ambiguous nimbus,
medallion of my ordeal.
No one crosses that circle.

Having been hanged for something
I never said,
I can now say anything I can say.

Holiness gleams on my dirty fingers,
I eat flowers and dung,
two forms of the same thing, I eat mice
and give thanks, blasphemies
gleam and burst in my wake
like lovely bubbles.
I speak in tongues,
my audience is owls.

My audience is God,
because who the hell else could understand me?
Who else has been dead twice?

The words boil out of me,
coil after coil of sinuous possibility.
The cosmos unravels from my mouth,
all fullness, all vacancy.

OWL BURNING

A few inches down and the soil stops
like a bolted door. A hard frost and that's that
for anything left unharvested.

Why should an old woman suck up the space,
the black roots, red juice that should be going
instead into the children?

Of course she practised magic.
When you're that hungry
you need such hooks and talons.

Held her breath at midnight, uncrossed her fingers,
and owls' feathers sprouted all over her
like mould on meat, but faster.

Saw her myself, hunting mice
in the moonlight. Silent
as the shadow of a hand thrown by a candle.

A good disguise, but I knew it was her
next day, by the white feather
caught in her hair.

She burned extremely, thick fat on fire.
Making grey screams. Giving back
to the air what she took when she shrivelled us.

She might have saved herself
with her white owl's voice
but we cut parts off her first

so she couldn't fly.
The fingers, those are the wings.
We watched her smoulder and got drunk after.

Her heart was the ember
we used to relight our stoves.
This is our culture,

no business of yours.
You have soft feet.
You don't know what it's like,
so close to bedrock.

My father chops with his axe
and the leaves fall off the trees.
It's nineteen forty-three.
He's splitting wood for the winter.
His gun leans behind the door,
beside his goose-greased workboots.
Smoke comes out of the metal chimney.

At night I sleep in a bunk bed.
The waves stroke the lake.
In the mornings it is so cold
we can see our breath
and the ice on the rocky shore.
My mother rakes the ashes
out from under the oven.

This is comfort and safety,
the sound of chopping in the empty forest,
the smell of smoke.
It's nineteen forty-three.
After it rains we have a bonfire.
The children dance around it,
singing about the war
which is happening elsewhere.
What has become of them, those words
that once shone with such
glossy innocence?
I rolled them in my mouth like marbles,
they tasted pure:
smoke, gun, boots, oven.
The fire. The scattered ashes. The winter forest.

I sit in a pink room;
the chest of drawers
has antique man-bored wormholes.

Isn't there enough of the past
without making more?

It's nineteen forty-three.
It's nineteen ninety-four,
I can hear the sound of the chopping.
It's because of the ocean,
it's because of the war
which won't stay under the waves and leaves.
The carpet smells of ashes.

This is the pink hotel
where everything recurs
and nothing is elsewhere.

Now see: they've found a man in a glacier,
two thousand years old, or three,
with everything intact: shoes, teeth, and arrows,
closed eyes, fur hat, the charm he wore to protect him
from death by snow. They think he must have been
a messenger, done in by bad weather,
and still fresh as a mastodon. Then there's

the box of slides in the cellar
my brother found, the kind we used to
tape between glass. As it turns out
the wrong thing for mildew.
Some cleaning, scraping away those little
flowers of crystallizing earth, and then
a wand of light, and here's my father,
alive or else preserved, younger than all
of us now, dark-haired and skinny,
in baggy trousers, woollen legs tucked into
those lace-up boots of our ancestors,
by a lake, feeding a picnic fire
in the clear blue-tinged air of either
a northern summer or else a film
of aging gelatin spread thinly
with fading colours,
the reds pushing towards pink, the greens greying,

but there. There still. This was all we got,
this echo, this freeze-framed
simulacrum or slight imprint,
in answer to our prayers for everlastingness,

the first time we discovered
we could not stop, or live backwards;
when we opened
our eyes, found we were rocked

with neither love nor malice in the ruthless
icy arms of Chemistry and Physics, our
bad godmothers. It was they
who were present at our birth, who laid
the curse on us: *You will not sleep forever.*

Right now I am the flower girl.
I bring fresh flowers,
dump out the old ones, the greenish water
that smells like dirty teeth
into the bathroom sink, snip off the stem ends
with surgical scissors I borrowed
from the nursing station,
put them into a jar
I brought from home, because they don't have vases
in this hotel for the ill,
place them on the table beside my father
where he can't see them
because he won't open his eyes.

He lies flattened under the white sheet.
He says he is on a ship,
and I can see it—
the functional white walls, the minimal windows,
the little bells, the rubbery footsteps of strangers,
the whispering all around
of the air-conditioner, or else the ocean,
and he is on a ship;
he's giving us up, giving up everything
but the breath going in
and out of his diminished body;
minute by minute he's sailing slowly away,
away from us and our waving hands
that do not wave.

The women come in, two of them, in blue;
it's no use being kind, in here,
if you don't have hands like theirs—
large and capable, the hands
of plump muscular angels,
the ones that blow trumpets and lift swords.

They shift him carefully, tuck in the corners.
It hurts, but as little as possible.
Pain is their lore. The rest of us
are helpless amateurs.

A suffering you can neither cure nor enter—
there are worse things, but not many.
After a while it makes us impatient.
Can't we do anything but feel sorry?

I sit there, watching the flowers
in their pickle jar. He is asleep, or not.

I think: He looks like a turtle.
Or: He looks erased.
But somewhere in there, at the far end of the tunnel
of pain and forgetting he's trapped in
is the same father I knew before,
the one who carried the green canoe
over the portage, the painter trailing,
myself with the fishing rods, slipping
on the wet boulders and slapping flies.
That was the last time we went there.

There will be a last time for this also,
bringing cut flowers to this white room.
Sooner or later I too
will have to give everything up,
even the sorrow that comes with these flowers,
even the anger,
even the memory of how I brought them
from a garden I will no longer have by then,
and put them beside my dying father,
hoping I could still save him.

Sitting at noon over the carrot salad
my sister and I compare dreams.

She says, Father was there
in some kind of very strange nightgown
covered with bristles, like a hair shirt.
He was blind, he was stumbling around
bumping into things, and I couldn't stop crying.

I say, Mine was close.
He was still alive, and all of it
was a mistake, but it was our fault.
He couldn't talk, but it was clear
he wanted everything back, the shoes, the binoculars
we'd given away or thrown out.
He was wearing stripes, like a prisoner.
We were trying to be cheerful,
but I wasn't happy to see him:
now we would have to do the whole thing over again.

Who sends us these messages,
oblique and muffled?
What good can they do?

In the daylight we know
what's gone is gone,
but at night it's different.
Nothing gets finished,
not dying, not mourning;
the dead repeat themselves, like clumsy drunks
lurching sideways through the doors
we open to them in sleep;
these slurred guests, never entirely welcome,
even those we have loved the most,
especially those we have loved the most,

returning from where we shoved them
away too quickly:
from under the ground, from under the water,
they clutch at us, they clutch at us,
we won't let go.

In the full moon you dream more.
I know where I am: the Ottawa River
far up, where the dam goes across.
Once, midstorm, in the wide cold water
upstream, two long canoes full
of children tipped, and they all held hands
and sang till the chill reached their hearts.
I suppose in our waking lives that's the best
we can hope for, if you think of that moment
stretched out for years.
                              Once, my father
and I paddled seven miles
along a lake near here
at night, with the trees like a pelt of dark
hackles, and the waves hardly moving.
In the moonlight the way ahead was clear
and obscure both. I was twenty
and impatient to get there, thinking
such a thing existed.
                              None of this
is in the dream, of course. Just the thick square-
edged shape of the dam, and eastward
the hills of sawdust from the mill, gleaming as white
as dunes. To the left, stillness; to the right,
the swirling foam of rapids
over sharp rocks and snags; and below that, my father,
moving away downstream
in his boat, so skilfully
although dead, I remember now; but no longer as old.
He wears his grey hat, and evidently
he can see again. There now,
he's around the corner. He's heading eventually
to the sea. Not the real one, with its sick whales
and oil slicks, but the other sea, where there can still be
safe arrivals.

Only a dream, I think, waking
to the sound of nothing.
Not nothing. I heard: it was a beach, or shore,
and someone far off, walking.
Nowhere familiar. Somewhere I've been before.
It always takes a long time
to decipher where you are.

VERMILION FLYCATCHER, SAN PEDRO RIVER, ARIZONA

The river's been here, violent, right where we're standing,
you can tell by the trash caught overhead in the trees.
Now it's a trickle, and we're up to our knees
in late-spring yellowing weeds. A vermilion
flycatcher darts down, flutters up, perches.
Stick a pin in your thumb, the bead of blood
would be his colour. He's filled with joy
and the tranced rage of sex. How he conjures,
with his cry like a needle. A punctuation. A bone button

on fire. Everything bad you can imagine
is happening somewhere else, or happened
here, a hundred years or centuries
ago. He sings, and there's the murder:
you see it, forming under
the shimmering air, a man with brown
or white skin lying reversed
in the vanished water, a spear
or bullet in his back. At the ford, where the deer
come at dusk to cross and drink
and be ambushed. The red bird

is sitting on the same tree, intensely
bright in the sun that gleams on cruelty, on broken
skullbone, arrow, spur. Vultures cluster,
he doesn't care. He and his other-coloured mate
ignore everything but their own rapture.
Who knows what they remember?
Birds never dream, being their own.
Dreams, I mean. As for you, the river
that isn't there is the same one
you could drown in, face down.

The moment when, after many years
of hard work and a long voyage
you stand in the centre of your room,
house, half-acre, square mile, island, country,
knowing at last how you got there,
and say, *I own this,*

is the same moment the trees unloose
their soft arms from around you,
the birds take back their language,
the cliffs fissure and collapse,
the air moves back from you like a wave
and you can't breathe.

No, they whisper. *You own nothing.*
You were a visitor, time after time
climbing the hill, planting the flag, proclaiming.
We never belonged to you.
You never found us.
It was always the other way round.

Walking through the ruins
on your way to work
that do not look like ruins
with the sunlight pouring over
the seen world
like hail or melted
silver, that bright
and magnificent, each leaf
and stone quickened and specific in it,
and you can't hold it,
you can't hold any of it. Distance surrounds you,
marked out by the ends of your arms
when they are stretched to their fullest.
You can go no farther than this,
you think, walking forward,
pushing the distance in front of you
like a metal cart on wheels
with its barriers and horizontals.
Appearance melts away from you,
the offices and pyramids
on the horizon shimmer and cease.
No one can enter that circle
you have made, that clean circle
of dead space you have made
and stay inside,
mourning because it is clean.

Then there's the girl, in the white dress,
meaning purity, or the failure
to be any colour. She has no hands, it's true.
The scream that happened to the air
when they were taken off
surrounds her now like an aureole
of hot sand, of no sound.
Everything has bled out of her.

Only a girl like this
can know what's happened to you.
If she were here she would
reach out her arms towards
you now, and touch you
with her absent hands
and you would feel nothing, but you would be
touched all the same.

FROM

THE DOOR

✦ ✦ ✦

Shivering in the almost-drizzle
inside the wooden outboard,
nose over gunwale,
I watched it drip and spread
on the sheenless water:

the brightest thing in wartime,
a slick of rainbow,
ephemeral as insect wings,
green, blue, red, and pink,
my shimmering private sideshow.

Was this my best toy, then?
This toxic smudge, this overspill
from a sloppy gascan filled
with essence of danger?

I knew that it was poison,
its beauty an illusion:
I could spell *flammable*.

But still, I loved the smell:
so alien, a whiff
of starstuff.

I would have liked to drink it,
inhale its iridescence.
As if I could.
That's how gods lived: *as if.*

We get too sentimental
over dead animals.
We turn maudlin.
But only those with fur,
only those who look like us,
at least a little.

Those with big eyes,
eyes that face front.
Those with smallish noses
or modest beaks.

No one laments a spider.
Nor a crab.
Hookworms rate no wailing.
Fish neither.
Baby seals make the grade,
and dogs, and sometimes owls.
Cats almost always.

Do we think they are like dead children?
Do we think they are a part of us,
the animal soul
stashed somewhere near the heart,
fuzzy and trusting,
and vital and on the prowl,
and brutal towards other forms of life,
and happy most of the time,
and also stupid?

(Why almost always cats? Why do dead cats
call up such ludicrous tears?
Why such deep mourning?
Because we can no longer
see in the dark without them?

Because we're cold
without their fur? Because we've lost
our hidden second skin,
the one we'd change into
when we wanted to have fun,
when we wanted to kill things
without a second thought,
when we wanted to shed the dull thick weight
of being human?)

My father, ninety years ago,
at the age of—my guess—ten,
walked three miles through the forest
on his way to school

along the sedgy wetfoot shore
of the brimming eel-filled rush-fringed
peat-brown river,
leaving a trail of jittering blackflies,
his hands already broad and deft
at the ends of his fraying sleeves.

Along this path he noticed
everything: mushroom and scat, wildbloom,
snail and iris, clubmoss, fern and cone.

It must have been an endless
breathing in: between
the wish to know and the need to praise
there was no seam.

One day he saw a drenched log floating
heavily downstream,
and on it a butterfly, blue as eyes.
This was the moment (I later heard)
that shot him off on his tangent

into the abstruse world
of microscopes and numbers,
lapel pins, cars, and wanderings,
away from the ten square miles
of logged-out bushlots
he never named as poverty,
and the brown meandering river
he was always in some way after that
trying in vain to get back to.

My mother dwindles and dwindles
and lives and lives.
Her strong heart drives her
as heedless as an engine
through one night after another.
Everyone says *This can't go on,*
but it does.
It's like watching somebody drown.

If she were a boat, you'd say
the moon shines through her ribs
and no one's steering,
yet she can't be said to be drifting;
somebody's in there.
Her blind eyes light her way.

Outside, in her derelict garden,
the weeds grow almost audibly:
nightshade, goldenrod, thistle.
Each time I hack them down
another wave spills forward,
up towards her window.
They batter the brick wall slowly,

muffle border and walkway,
slurring her edges.
Her old order of words
collapses in on itself.
Today, after weeks of silence,
she made a sentence:
I don't think so.

I hold her hand, I whisper,
Hello, hello.
If I said *Goodbye* instead,

if I said, *Let go,*
what would she do?

But I can't say it.
I promised to see this through,
whatever that may mean.
What can I possibly tell her?
I'm here.
I'm here.

CRICKETS

September. Wild aster. Fox grapes,
tiny and bitter,
the indigo taste of winter
already blooming inside them.

The house is invaded by crickets,
they've come inside for the warmth.
They creep into the stove
and behind the refrigerator,
make sorties across the floor,
singing to one another:
Here, here, here, here.
We step on them by mistake,
or pick them up, dozens of them,
dozens of wriggling black consciences,
and throw them out the door.

There's nothing for them to eat,
not with us. No more harvests or granaries,
only tables and chairs.
We have become too affluent.
Inside, they'd die of hunger.
Wait, wait, wait, wait, they say. They fear
they'll freeze. Under the broom
their dark armour crackles.

The ant and the grasshopper have
their places in our bestiaries:
the first stows wealth, the second
spends. We hold the middle ground, approve
the ant (head), love
the (heart) grasshopper,
emulate both: why choose?
We hoard and fiddle.

As for the crickets, they've
been censored. We have
no crickets on our hearths. We have no hearths.

Nevertheless, they wake us
at cold midnight,
small timid voices we can't locate,
small watches ticking away,
cheap ones; small tin mementoes:
late, late, late, late,
somewhere in the bedsheets,
in the bedsprings, in the ear,
the hordes of the starved dead
come back as our heartbeats.

HEART

Some people sell their blood. You sell your heart.
It was either that or the soul.
The hard part is getting the damn thing out.
A kind of twisting motion, like shucking an oyster,
your spine a wrist,
and then, hup! it's in your mouth.
You turn yourself partially inside out
like a sea anemone coughing a pebble.
There's a broken plop, the racket
of fish guts into a pail,
and there it is, a huge glistening deep-red clot
of the still-alive past, whole on the plate.

It gets passed around. It's slithery. It gets dropped,
but also tasted. Too coarse, says one. Too salty.
Too sour, says another, making a face.
Each one is an instant gourmet,
and you stand listening to all this
in the corner, like a newly hired waiter,
your diffident, skilful hand on the wound hidden
deep in your shirt and chest,
shyly, heartless.

Time for gardening again; for poetry; for arms
up to the elbows in leftover
deluge, hands in the dirt, groping around
among the rootlets, bulbs, lost marbles, blind
snouts of worms, cat droppings, your own future
bones, whatever's down there
supercharged, a dim glint in the darkness.
When you stand on bare earth in your bare feet
and the lightning whips through you, two ways
at once, they say you are grounded,
and that's what poetry is: a hot wire.
You might as well stick a fork
in a wall socket. So don't think it's just about flowers.
Though it is, in a way.
You spent this morning among the bloodsucking
perennials, the billowing peonies,
the lilies building to outburst,
the leaves of the foxgloves gleaming like hammered
copper, the static crackling among the spiny columbines.
Scissors, portentous trowel, the wheelbarrow
yellow and inert, the grassblades
whispering like ions. You think it wasn't all working
up to something? You ought to have worn rubber
gloves. Thunder budding in the spires of lupins,
their clumps and updrafts, pollen and resurrection
unfolding from each restless nest
of petals. Your arms hum, the hair
stands up on them; just one touch and you're struck.
It's too late now, the earth splits open,
the dead rise, purblind and stumbling
in the clashing of last-day daily
sunlight, furred angels crawl
all over you like swarming bees, the maple
trees above you shed their deafening keys
to heaven, your exploding
syllables litter the lawn.

So here we are again, my dear,
on the same shore we set out from
years ago, when we were promising,
but minus—now—a lot of hair,
or fur or feathers, whatever.
I like the bifocals. They make you look
even more like an owl than you are.
I suppose we've both come far. But

how far are we truly, from where we started,
under the fresh-laid moon, when we plotted
to astound? When we thought
something of meaning could still be done
by singing, or won, like trophies.
I took the fences, you the treetops, where we
hooted and yowled our carnivorous
fervid hearts out, and see,
we did get prizes: there they are,
a scroll, a gold watch, and a kissoff
handshake from the stand-in
for the Muse, who couldn't come herself,
but sent regrets. Now we can say

flattering things about each other
on dust jackets. Whatever
made us think we could change the world?
Us and our clever punct-
uation marks. A machine-gun, now—
that would be different. No more unct-
uous adjectives. Cut straight to the verb.
Ars longa, mors brevissima. The life
of poetry breeds the lust
for action, of the most ordinary
sort. Whacking the heads off dandelions,
or bats or bureaucrats,
smashing car windows. Though

at least we've been tolerated,
or even celebrated—which meant
a brief caper in the transient glare
of the sawdust limelight,
and your face used later for fishwrap—
but most of the time ignored
by this crowd that has finally admitted
to itself it doesn't give
much of a fart for art,
and would rather see a good evisceration
any day. You might as well have been
a dentist, as your father hoped. You

want attention, still? Take your clothes off
at a rush-hour stoplight, howl obscenities,
or shoot someone. You'll get
your name in the paper, maybe,
for what it's worth. In any case

where do we both get off?
Is this small talent we have prized
so much, and rubbed like silver
spoons, until it shone
at least as brightly as neon, really
so much better than the ability
to win the sausage-eating contest,
or juggle six plates at once?
What's the use anyway
of calling the dead back, moving stones,
or making animals cry? I

think of you, loping along at night
to the convenience store, to buy your pint
of milk, your six medium eggs,
your head stuffed full of consonants
like lovely pebbles
you picked up on some lustrous beach
you can't remember—my feather-

headed fool, what have you got
in your almost-empty pockets
that would lure even the lowliest mugger?
Who needs your handful
of glimmering air, your foxfire, your few
underwater crystal tricks
that work only in moonlight?
Noon hits them and they fall apart,
old bones and earth, old teeth, a bundleful
of shadow. Sometimes, I know, the almost-holy
whiteness rooted in our skulls spreads out
like thistles in a vacant lot, a hot powdery
flare-up, which is not a halo
and will return at intervals
if we're grateful or else lucky, and
will end by fusing our neurons. Yet
singing's a belief
we can't give up.
Anything can become a saint
if you pray to it enough—
spaceship, teacup, wolf—
and what we want is intercession,
that iridescent ribbon
that once held song to object.
We feel everything hovering
on the verge of becoming itself:
the tree is almost a tree, the dog
pissing against it won't be a dog
unless we notice it
and call it by its name: "Here, dog."
And so we stand on balconies and rocky
hilltops, and caterwaul our best,
and the world flickers
in and out of being,
and we think it needs our permission. We

shouldn't flatter ourselves: really
it's the other way around. We're at

the mercy of any stray
rabid mongrel or thrown stone or cancerous
ray, or our own
bodies: we were born with mortality's
hook in us, and year by year it drags us
where we're going: down. But

surely there is still
a job to be done by us, at least
time to be passed; for instance, we could
celebrate inner beauty. Gardens.
Love and desire. Lust. Children. Social justice
of various kinds. Include fear and war.
Describe what it is to be tired. Now
we're getting there. But this is much
too pessimistic! Hey, we've got
each other, and a roof, and regular
breakfasts! Cream and mice! For

our sort, elsewhere, it's often worse:
a heaved boot, poisoned meat, or dragged
by the wings or tail off to some wall
or trench and forced to kneel
and have your brains blown out, splattering all over
that Nature we folks are so keen on—
in the company of a million others,
let it be said—
and in the name of what? What noun?
What god or state? The world becomes
one huge deep vowel of horror,
while behind those mildewed flags, the slogans
that always rhyme with *dead,*
sit a few old guys making money. So

honestly. Who wants to hear it?
Last time I did that number, honey,
the audience was squirrels.
But I don't need to tell you.

The worst is, now we're respectable.
We're in anthologies. We're taught in schools,
with cleaned-up biographies and skewed photos.
We're part of the mug show now.
In ten years, you'll be on a stamp,
where anyone at all can lick you. Ah

well, my dear, our leaky cardboard
gondola has brought us this far,
us and our paper guitar.
No longer semi-immortal, but moulting owl
and arthritic pussycat, we row
out past the last protecting
sandbar, towards the salty
open sea, the dogs'-head gate,
and after that, oblivion.
But sing on, sing
on, someone may still be listening
besides me. The fish for instance.
Anyway, my dearest one,
we still have the moon.

The singer of owls wandered off into the darkness.
Once more he had not won a prize.
It was like that at school.
He preferred dim corners, camouflaged himself
with the hair and ears of the others,
and thought about long vowels, and hunger,
and the bitterness of deep snow.
Such moods do not attract glitter.

What is it about me? he asked the shadows.
By this time they were shadows of trees.
Why have I wasted my lifeline?
I opened myself to your silences.
I allowed ruthlessness
and feathers to possess me.
I swallowed mice.
Now, when I'm at the end, and emptied
of words, and breathless,
you didn't help me.

Wait, said the owl soundlessly.
Among us there are no prices.
You sang out of necessity,
as I do. You sang for me,
and my thicket, my moon, my lake.
Our song is a night song.
Few are awake.

THE LAST RATIONAL MAN

In the reign of Caligula

The last rational man takes his old seat in the Senate.
He's not sure why he's still here.
He must be on some list or other.
Last year there were many more like him,
but they've been picked off one by one.
He bathes daily, and practises slow breathing
and the doctrines of Stoicism.
Lose your calm, he reminds himself,
and you will lose everything.
Nevertheless he's getting tired.
The effort of saying nothing is wearing him down.
The others in their rich men's outfits
banter carefully, sticking to topics
that grow fewer in number; even the weather
is perilous, the sun too,
since the Emperor claims to control the one
and to be the other.

Here he comes now, with his chittering retinue
of paid retainers twitchy with bonhomie;
he's gilded and bright as a chariot in false taste,
and just returned from a fresh triumph.
With a grin he lifts his gleaming finger:
baskets of shells cascade onto the floor,
and the room stinks of dead molluscs.
Look, says the Emperor, *it's treasure!*
By the power of my supreme divinity
I've defeated the King of the Sea!
His eyes hold the malicious glitter
of a madman who's telling a lie,
and knows it, and dares contradiction.

The others cheer. The last rational man
forces himself to cheer also.
The Emperor's gaze is boring a hole
through the bellowing air straight towards him.
Then they lead in the Emperor's horse,
wreathed in garlands like a belly dancer.
I'm making him a Senator!
trills the Emperor. *Greet your new brother!*

The last rational man finds himself rising.
As he opens his mouth he can see
the red bathwater, his own slit wrists,
his house robbed, his sons headless.
That's only a horse, he says.
The words hang there
hopelessly, like the banners of a city
already defeated, given over to pillagers.
In what way, thinks the last rational man,
can such a place be said, still, to exist?

Silence crystallizes
around his head like a halo of ice.
He stands there.
No one looks at him except the Emperor,
who smiles at him with something almost like pity.

The dead woman thrown down on the dusty road
is very beautiful.
One leg extended, the other flexed, foot pointed
towards the knee, the arm flung overhead, the hand
relaxed into a lovely gesture
a dancer might well study for years
and never attain.
Her purple robe is shaped
as if it's fluttering;
her head is turned away.

There are other dead people scattered around
like trees blown over,
left in the wake of frightened men
battering their way to some huge purpose
they can't now exactly remember,

But it's this beautiful woman who holds me,
dancing there on the ground
with such perfection.

Oh dead beautiful woman, if anyone
had the power to wrench me through despair
and arid helplessness
into the heart of prayer,
it would be you—

Instead I'll make for you
the only thing I can:
although I'll never know your name,
I won't ever forget you.
Look: on the dusty ground
under my hand, on this cheap grey paper,
I'm placing a small stone, here:

o

THE VALLEY OF THE HERETICS

Luberon Valley, Provence

This is the valley of the heretics: once far
away from everything, now overrun
by the forces of invasion, ourselves included.
In our metal shell we're off to see the sights:
a green river; a hundred-year-old fountain
with a sly-eyed naked girl reclined in stone
underpinning the town's notables; the rows
of flapping scarves and aprons; trestle tables
with bric-a-brac—chess sets and salt cellars
left over from vanished households, plaster
cicadas labelled "artisan," probably made in Taiwan.

We're not there yet. We fight our way through the air
while the reed beds and bushes thrash as if pounded.
The dry wind hurtles down on us; torn plastic
bags like ectoplasmic birds flitter and stream,
and gusts buffet the sign showing a big red blood drop
with white gloves and a grin, and the other poster,
a girl in underwear licking her lips and smirking.
These would have been sinister magic
once, anywhere icons were rife, but especially here
between the secretive mountains, this harsh
rock-strewn place infected with goats and sorcery.

As we rush through clouds of the scouring dust
that puffs into the car and powders our hair,
fine lines race across our faces
like speeded-up films of neglected frescoes.
The heretics, holed up in their hilltop towns,
taught that the body was trash,
the earth was made by a lesser, malignant god—
for which thoughts they were set on fire, and burned

in anguish. We wish not to believe them
but on windy days like this we breathe them in
with unease, a sense of foreboding:
their ashes are everywhere.

Here's Joan in her penitential bedsheet,
peeled of her armour, hair shorn,
wrapped round with string
like a boned rolled leg of lamb,

topped with a hat that looks like paper,
newspaper at that, but without the print,
a conical dunce cap.
Everything pale, hands, bare feet,
thin vestment, drained and blank,
white as the centre of a flare:
foreknowledge does that.

Some cleric putting a match to her.
Neither of them looks happy about it.
Once lit, she'll burn like a book,
like a book that was never finished,
like a locked-up library.

Her two left-handed angels
and the ardent catchwords
they whispered into her ear—
Courage! Forward! King!
will burn as well.
Their voices will shrivel and blow away
in a scrawl of ash,

charred scraps of a dirty joke
in the long and dissolute narrative
people keep telling themselves about God,
and the watchers in the square will cheer,
incinerating her with their eyes,
since everyone likes a good bonfire
and a nice cry, some time afterwards.

It's you reading her now,
reading the Book of Joan.
What do you make of her?
Joan, the cocksure messenger,
or lunatic, or glassy sphere
containing a pure, terse chapter
of a story with both ends missing?

You'll patch up some translation,
you and your desk-lamp lightbulb,
you and your white-hot stare.

THEY GIVE EVIDENCE

After a room-sized installation by Dadang Christanto, 1996

They give evidence
in an empty room
sixteen of them, eight men, eight women,
four rows of four,
unlucky number.

They are all bald,
they are all naked,
they all have wide shoulders,
huge hands, strong legs, huge feet.

Their skin is greyish white,
greyish brown,
mineral colours, dusty and scarred
as if they have been buried;
as if they have been buried a long time
and secretly dug up, like ancient sculptures
guarding the bones of kings;
as if they have been dead.

But they are not dead exactly.
Their mouths are open, although there are no tongues;
their eyes are open, although there are no eyes;
they have the spaces for tongues and eyes,
empty spaces;
they are speaking and looking
with this emptiness they carry.

They carry emptiness,
they carry empty clothing.
Coloured and patterned, not faded,
red yellow blue, shirts blouses trousers,
moulded in the shapes of bodies,
the bodies cloth once held.

Men and women, and children
four children, five
children, six,
it's hard to tell.

Those who are naked carry the clothes
that never have been theirs.
They carry the clothes gently
as if the clothes are asleep,
as if the vanished bodies inside the clothes are sleeping,
the bodies of air.
Gently, they hold out the stiff empty clothing
like frozen garlands now, like offerings.
Like unfortunate flowers.

They speak words, I think.
They testify.
They name names.
That's what you'd assume.

Or perhaps it's a chant,
a prayer a question.
Perhaps they are singing praises.

To whom are they chanting and praying?
Who are they questioning?

The wall they face is blank.
Whose praises do they sing?

Perhaps they are angels
of a new kind, bald and eyeless
and without wings.
Angels are messengers.
Perhaps they bring a message.
The messages of angels
are seldom lucky.

(What are the names?)

You could sit on your chair and pick over the language
as if it were a bowl of peas.
A lot of people do that.
It might be instructive.
You don't even need the chair,
you could juggle plates of air.

You could poke sticks through the chain-link fence
at your brain, which you keep locked up in there,
which crouches and sulks like an old tortoise,
and glares out at you, sluggish and eyeless.
You could tease it that way,
make it blunder and think,
and emit a croaking sound
you could call truth.
A harmless activity,
sort of like knitting,
until you go too far with it
and they bring out the nooses and matches.

Or you could do something else.
Something more sociable.
More group-oriented.
A lot of people do that too.
They like the crowds and the screaming,
they like the adrenalin.

Hunker down. Get a blackout curtain.
Pretend you're not home.
Pretend you're deaf and dumb.
Look: pitchforks and torches!
Judging from old pictures,
things could get worse.

Go to the mouth of a cave,
dig a trench, slit the throat
of an animal, pour out the blood.

Or sit in a chair
with others, at a round table
in a darkened room.
Close your eyes, hold hands.

These techniques might be called
the heroic and the mezzotint.
We aren't sure we believe in either,

or in the dead, when they do appear,
smelling like damp hair,
flickering like faulty toasters,
rustling their tissue paper
faces, their sibilants, their fissures,
trailing their fraudulent gauze.

Their voices are dry as lentils
falling into a glass jar.
Why can't they speak up clearly
instead of mumbling about keys and numbers,
and stairs, they mention stairs . . .

Why do we keep pestering them?
Why do we insist they love us?
What did we want to ask them
anyway? Nothing they wish to tell.

Or stand by a well or pool
and drop in a pebble.
The sound you hear is the question
you should have asked.

Also the answer.

I show you a girl running at night
among trees that do not love her
and the shadows of many fathers

without paths, without even
torn bread or white stones
under a moon that says nothing to her.
I mean it says: *Nothing*.

There is a man nearby
who claims he is a lover
but smells of plunder.
How many times will he have to tell her
to kill herself before she does?

It's no use to say
to this girl: You are well cared for.
Here is a safe room, here
is food and everything you need.

She cannot see what you see.
The darkness washes towards her
like an avalanche. Like falling.
She would like to step forward into it
as if it were not a vacancy
but a destination,
leaving her body pulled off
and crumpled behind her like a sleeve.

I am the old woman
found always in stories like this one,
who says, *Go back, my dear.*

Back is into the cellar
where the worst is,

where the others are,
where you can see
what you would look like dead
and who wants it.

Then you will be free
to choose. To make
your way.

BOAT SONG

The Titanic

There's pushing and scrabbling,
not nearly enough lifeboats:
that much is obvious;

so why not spend the last few moments
practising our modest art
as we have always done,

creating a pool of possibly false comfort
in the midst of tragedy?
There's something to be said for it.

Picture us then in the ship's orchestra.
We all stay in our places,
tootling and strumming and marking time

with our workaday instruments
as the shouts and boots trample past.
Some have jumped; their furs and desperations

weigh them down. Clawed hands reach up through the ice.
What are we playing? Is it a waltz?
There's too much uproar

for the others to make it out clearly,
or else they're too far away—
an upbeat foxtrot, a sugary old hymn?

Whatever it is, that's us with the violins
as the lights fade and the great ship slides down
and the water closes in.

How did I get so dutiful? Was I always that way?
Going around as a child with a small broom and dustpan,
sweeping up dirt I didn't make,
or out into the yard with a stunted rake,
weeding the gardens of others
—the dirt blew back, the weeds flourished, despite my efforts—
and all the while with a frown of disapproval
for other people's fecklessness, and my own slavery.
I didn't perform these duties willingly.
I wanted to be on the river, or dancing,
but something had me by the back of the neck.
That's me too, years later, a purple-eyed wreck,
because whatever had to be finished wasn't, and I stayed late,
grumpy as a snake, on too much coffee,
and further on still, those groups composed of mutterings
and scoldings, and the set-piece exhortation:
Somebody ought to do something!
That was my hand shooting up.

But I've resigned. I've ditched the grip of my echo.
I've decided to wear sunglasses, and a necklace
adorned with the gold word NO,
and eat flowers I didn't grow.
Still, why do I feel so responsible
for the wailing from shattered houses,
for birth defects and unjust wars,
and the soft, unbearable sadness
filtering down from distant stars?

Disturbed earth: some plants sprout quickly in it.
Sow thistles come to mind.
After you've wrenched them out
they'll snake back underground
and thrust their fleshy prickled snouts in
where you intended hostas.

Hawkweed will do that. Purslane. Purple vetch.
Marginals, hugging ditches,
flagrant with seed,
strewing their paupers' bouquets.

Why is it you reject them,
them and their tangled harmonies
and raffish madrigals?
Because they thwart your will.

I feel the same about them:
I hack and dig,
I stomp their pods and stems,
I slash and crush them. Still,

suppose I make a comeback—
a transmutation, say—
once I've been spaded under?
Some quirky growth or ambush?

Don't search the perennial border:
look for me in disturbed earth.

This is a tiny language,
smaller than Gallic;
when you have your boots on
you scarcely see it.

A dry scorched dialect
with many words for holding on,
and with grey branches
like an old tree's, brittle and leafless.

In the rain they go leathery,
then sly, like rubber.
They send up their little mouths
on stems, red-lipped and round,

each one pronouncing the same syllable,
o, o, o, like the dumbfounded
eyes of minnows.
Thousands of spores, of rumours

infiltrating the fissures,
moving unnoticed into
the ponderous *is* of the boulder,
breaking down rock.

Off we go, unsteadily down the gangway,
bundled up in our fleecy layers,
mittened like infants, breasting—as they
once said—the icy waves
in our inner tube of a boat,
so full of pills we rattle.

We're what the French politely call
the Third Age: One and Two behind us, Four
still tactfully not mentioned, though
it looms. It's the one after.
Meanwhile, we scream full throttle
as the spray hits us,
delighted to be off the hook.
Not responsible.

Aaju is one of our minders—
she's got her sealskin parka on
for the camera folk, toting her bear gun.
She gives us a strict look, sideways:
she's seen too many like us
to find us truly droll.
Herding us will be like herding
lemmings. We'll wander off.
Plus, we don't listen.

We've bumbled ashore now. Time for lessons.
Jane's up today. She says:
When you see a creek like this one,
flowing into a bay,
and there's flat land for a tent,
and a view of the sea, for hunting,
and berry bushes, a hillside full,
you know there must have been people.

And sure enough, see here:
a ring of stones, a fox trap,
and farther on, a grave,
thick slabs to keep out the animals.
They like it when you visit them,
says Aaju. *Just say hello.*

So we lie down on the soft moss, gaze up
at the sky marbled with cloud
and a raven circling, and it's total peace
among the voices that do not speak,

except we can't stay here:
we need to do more real life,
see the thing through. So back we amble
in our clumsy boots and Gore-tex windgear,
trundling over the boulders
like huge old children called back to school.

Aaju's perched on a distant hill
to keep us harm-free.
She stands on one foot, lifts her arms,
a silent message:
Hello! I'm here!
    Here is where I am.
I stand on one foot, too.

You heard the man you love
talking to himself in the next room.
He didn't know you were listening.
You put your ear against the wall
but you couldn't catch the words,
only a kind of rumbling.
Was he angry? Was he swearing?
Or was it some kind of commentary
like a long obscure footnote on a page of poetry?
Or was he trying to find something he'd lost,
such as the car keys?
Then suddenly he began to sing.
You were startled
because this was a new thing,
but you didn't open the door, you didn't go in,
and he kept on singing, in his deep voice, off-key,
a purple-green monotone, dense and heathery.
He wasn't singing for you, or about you.
He had some other source of joy,
nothing to do with you at all—
he was an unknown man, singing in his own room, alone.
Why did you feel so hurt then, and so curious,
and also happy,
and also set free?

The old people descend the hill in slow motion.
It's a windy hill,
a hill of treacheries and pebbles,
and twisted ankles.

One has a stick, one not.
Their clothing is bizarre,
though wash and wear.

Foot over foot they go,
down the eroded slope,
flapping like sails.
They want to get down to the ocean,
and they accomplish this.

(Could it be that we are the old people
already?
Surely not.
Not with such hats.)

We may have been here before;
at least it looks familiar,
but we are drawn to hills like these,
remote, bleak, old history,
nothing but stones.

Down by the tidal pool
there are two plastic bottles
a few small molluscs.

One person pees in a corner
out of the sun,
the other, not.

At this point, once, there might have been sex
with the waves rampaging in
as if in films.

But we stay fully clothed,
talk about rocks:
how did it get this way, the mix
of igneous and sandstone?
There's mica too, that glitter.

It's not sad. It's bright
and clear.
See how spryly we climb back up,
one claw and then the other.

The door swings open,
you look in.
It's dark in there,
most likely spiders:
nothing you want.
You feel scared.
The door swings closed.

The full moon shines,
it's full of delicious juice;
you buy a purse,
the dance is nice.
The door opens
and swings closed so quickly
you don't notice.

The sun comes out,
you have swift breakfasts
with your husband, who is still thin;
you wash the dishes,
you love your children,
you read a book,
you go to the movies.
It rains moderately.

The door swings open,
you look in:
why does this keep happening now?
Is there a secret?
The door swings closed.

The snow falls,
you clear the walk while breathing heavily;
it's not as easy as once.
Your children telephone sometimes.

The roof needs fixing.
You keep yourself busy.
The spring arrives.

The door swings open:
it's dark in there,
with many steps going down.
But what is that shining?
Is it water?
The door swings closed.

The dog has died.
This happened before.
You got another;
not this time though.
Where is your husband?
You gave up the garden.
It became too much.
At night there are blankets;
nonetheless you are wakeful.

The door swings open:
O god of hinges,
god of long voyages,
you have kept faith.
It's dark in there.
You confide yourself to the darkness.
You step in.
The door swings closed.

FROM

DEARLY

✦ ✦ ✦

These are the late poems.
Most poems are late
of course: too late,
like a letter sent by a sailor
that arrives after he's drowned.

Too late to be of help, such letters,
and late poems are similar.
They arrive as if through water.

Whatever it was has happened:
the battle, the sunny day, the moonlit
slipping into lust, the farewell kiss. The poem
washes ashore like flotsam.

Or late, as in late for supper:
all the words cold or eaten.
Scoundrel, plight, and vanquished,
or linger, bide, awhile,
forsaken, wept, forlorn.
Love and joy, even: thrice-gnawed songs.
Rusted spells. Worn choruses.

It's late, it's very late;
too late for dancing.
Still, sing what you can.
Turn up the light: sing on,
sing: On.

Cats suffer from dementia too. Did you know that?
Ours did. Not the black one, smart enough
to be neurotic and evade the vet.
The other one, the furrier's muff, the piece of fluff.
She'd writhe around on the sidewalk
for chance pedestrians, whisker
their trousers, though not when she started losing
what might have been her mind. She'd prowl the night
kitchen, taking a bite
from a tomato here, a ripe peach there,
a crumpet, a softening pear.
Is this what I'm supposed to eat?
Guess not. But what? But where?
Then up the stairs she'd come, moth-footed,
owl-eyed, wailing
like a tiny, fuzzy steam train: *Ar-woo! Ar-woo!*
So witless and erased. *O, who?*
Clawing at the bedroom door
shut tight against her. *Let me in,*
enclose me, tell me who I was.
No good. No purring. No contentment. Out
into the darkened cave of the dining room,
then in, then out, forlorn.
And when I go that way, grow fur, start howling,
scratch at your airwaves:
no matter who I claim I am
or how I love you,
turn the key. Bar the window.

We save them, as we save those curls
culled from our kids' first haircuts, or from lovers
felled too early. Here are

all of mine, safe in a file, their corners
clipped, each page engraved
with trips I barely remember.

Why was I wandering from there to there
to there? God only knows.
And the procession of wraiths' photos

claiming to prove that I was me:
the faces greyish discs, the fisheyes
trapped in the noonhour flashflare

with the sullen jacklit stare
of a woman who's just been arrested.
Sequenced, these pics are like a chart

of moon phases fading to blackout; or
like a mermaid doomed to appear onshore
every five years, and each time altered

to something a little more dead:
skin withering in the parching air,
marooned hair thinning as it dries,
cursed if she smiles or cries.

COCONUT

There were more things to buy right after the war.
Oranges made a comeback
and black and white morphed into rainbow.
Not yet avocados,

though suddenly, in the slack tide
of winter, in our cellar,
a coconut materialized
like the round hard hairy breast
of some wooden sasquatch.

Why the cellar?
That's where the axe was.

We drove a long steel nail
into each of the three soft eyes
and drained out the sweetish water.
Then we stood the globe on a block
and hacked it apart.

The pieces clattered over the floor,
which was not clean back then
in the age of coal and cinders.

First taste of sheer ambrosia!
Though mixed with ash and the shards of destruction
as Heaven always is, if you read the texts closely.

On the flannel sheet
in the pose of a deadman's float,
face down. The hands descend,
ignore the skin,
the xylophone of spine,
evade the blobs and lobes,
head for deep tissue,

go for the little hinges
that creak like tiny frogs—
twang the catgut strings
of the tight bruised tendons.

How rusted shut I am,
how locked, how oxidized.
Old baked-beans can,
Tin Woodwoman left in the rain.
Movement equals pain.
How corroded.

Who was it used to complain
he didn't have a brain?
Some straw-man cloth boy.

Me, it's the heart:
that's the part lacking.
I used to want one:
a dainty cushion of red silk
dangling from a blood ribbon,
fit for sticking pins in.
But I've changed my mind.
Hearts hurt.

I.

Too many people talk about what she should wear
so she will be fashionable, or at least
so she will not be killed.

Women have moved in next door
wrapped in pieces of cloth
that lack approval.

They're setting a bad example.
Get out the stones.

II.

Fur is an issue too:
her own and some animal's.
Once the world was nearly stripped of feathers,
all in the cause of headgear.

What was it for, my love,
this ripoff of the birds?
Once there was nothing she wouldn't do
to render herself alluring.
So many items attached to her head:
ribbons and ships, all curling.

Now her torso lies in the ditch
like a lost glove, like a tossed book
mostly unsaid. Unread.
In the high palace of words, one princess the less.

III.

Oh beware,
uncover your hair
or else they will burn down your castle.
Wait a minute: Cover it!
Hair. So controversial.

IV.

As for feet, they were always a problem.
Toes, heels, and ankles
take turns being obscene.
Little glass slippers, the better to totter.

Many things that are not what you want
arrive in the disguise of flowers.
Lotus foot, the petals
broken bones.

V.

Wool worn next to the skin
was once an army decree.
In mid-battle it's hard to shower.
Wool deterred microbes and did not stink,
or not as much. That was the theory.
Here you go: cashmere!
But armpits: drawbacks, damp as a groin,
even if pink:
not feminine.

VI.

Cotton on the other hand
was crackly. Still is.
Avoid it when making recordings.

You don't want it messing with the ghost voice
of yourself you leave behind in the air.

VII.

Silk, however,
is best for shrouds.
That's where it comes from, silk:
those seven veils the silkworms keep spinning,
hoping they will be butterflies.
Then they get boiled, and then unscrolled.

It's what you hope too, right?
That beyond death, there's flight?
After the shrouding, up you'll rise,
delicate wings and all. Oh honey,
it won't be like that.
Not quite.

When you stumble across your lover and your friend
naked in or on your bed
there are things that might be said.

Goodbye is not one of them.
You'll never close that clumsily opened door,
they'll be stuck in that room forever.

But did they have to be so naked?
So minus grace?
Floundering around as if in a spring puddle?

The legs too spindly, the waists too thick,
the flubbers here and there,
the tufts of hair . . .

Yes, it was a betrayal,
but not of you.
Only of some idea you'd had

of them, soft-lit and mystic,
with snowfall sifting down
and a mauve December sunset—

not this gauche flash,
this flesh akimbo,
caught in the glare of your stare.

FRIDA KAHLO, SAN MIGUEL, ASH WEDNESDAY

You faded so long ago
but here in the souvenir arcade
you're everywhere:
the printed cotton bags, the pierced tin boxes,
the scarlet T-shirts, the beaded crosses;
your coiled braids, your level stare,
your body of a deer or martyr.

It's a meme you can turn into
if your ending's strange enough
and ardent, and involves much pain.
The rope of a hanged man brings good luck;
saints dangle upside down
or offer their breasts on a plate
and we wear them, we invoke them,
insert them between our flesh and danger.

Fireworks, two streets over.
Something's burning somewhere,
or did burn, once.
A torn silk veil, a yellowing letter:
I'm dying here.
Love on a skewer,
a heart in flames.
We breathe you in, thin smoke,
grief in the form of ashes.

Yesterday the children smashed
their hollowed eggs on the heads of others,
baptizing them with glitter.
Shell fragments litter the park
like the wings of crushed butterflies,
like sand, like confetti:
azure, sunset, blood,
your colours.

What if I didn't want all that—
what he prophesied I could do
while coming to no good
and making my name forever?
Dye my hair black, pierce my face,
spew out fuckshaped energy,
hook up, kick back.
Wallow in besmirching fame.

What if I said No Thank You
to Mr. Musician God,
to sex for favours?
What if I stayed right here?
Right in my narrowing hometown
(which will later be burned down)
thinking of others first
and being manless and pitiable?
I'd have a dark-blue leather purse,
and crochet cotton gifts
—dolls' hats, toilet-roll covers—
the nieces would throw out later.
Then I could cry about failure,
pale, sere, minor.

At least I would not be brazen,
like a shield maiden, like a fender.
At least I would not be brash
and last seen alive
that day in mid-November
at the gas station, shivering, hitching,
in the dusk, just before

Someone wants your body.

What's the deal?
Beg, borrow, buy, or steal?
Gutter or pedestal?
That's how it is with bodies
that someone wants.

What's it worth to you?
A rose, a diamond,
a cool million, a joke, a drink?
The fiction that this one likes you?

You could bestow it, this body,
like the generous creature you are,
or blackout and have it snatched
and you'd never know.

Kiss it goodbye, the body
that was once yours.
It's off and running,
it's rolled in furs, it's dancing
or bleeding out in a meadow.

You didn't need it anyway,
it attracted too much attention.
Better with only a shadow.

Someone wants your shadow.

SONGS FOR MURDERED SISTERS

A cycle for baritone

1. EMPTY CHAIR

Who was my sister
Is now an empty chair

Is no longer,
Is no longer there

She is now emptiness
She is now air

2. ENCHANTMENT

If this were a story
I was telling my sister

A troll from the mountain
Would have stolen her

Or else a twisted magician
Turned her to stone

Or locked her in a tower
Or hidden her deep inside a golden flower

I would have to travel
West of the moon, east of the sun

To find the answer;
I'd speak the charm

And she'd be standing there
Alive and happy, come to no harm

But this is not a story.
Not that kind of story . . .

3. ANGER

Anger is red
The colour of spilled blood

He was all anger,
The man you tried to love

You opened the door
And death was standing there

Red death, red anger
Anger at you

For being so alive
And not destroyed by fear

What do you want? you said.
Red was the answer.

4. DREAM

When I sleep you appear
I am a child then
And you are young and still my sister

And it is summer;
I don't know the future,
Not in my dream

I'm going away, you tell me
On a long journey.
I have to go away.

No, stay, I call to you
As you grow smaller:
Stay here with me and play!

But suddenly I'm older
And it's cold and moonless
And it is winter . . .

5. BIRD SOUL

If birds are human souls
What bird are you?
A spring bird with a joyful song?
A high flyer?

Are you an evening bird
Watching the moon
Singing Alone, Alone,
Singing Dead Too Soon?

Are you an owl,
Soft-feathered predator?
Are you hunting, restlessly hunting
The soul of your murderer?

I know you are not a bird,
Though I know you've flown
So far, so far away.
I need you to be somewhere . . .

6. LOST

So many sisters lost
So many lost sisters

Over the years, thousands of years
So many sent away

Too soon into the night
By men who thought they had the right

Rage and hatred
Jealousy and fear

So many sisters killed
Over the years, thousands of years

Killed by fearful men
Who wanted to be taller

Over the years, thousands of years
So many sisters lost

So many tears . . .

7. RAGE

I was too late,
Too late to save you.

I feel the rage and pain
In my own fingers,

In my own hands
I feel the red command

To kill the man who killed you:
That would be only fair:

Him stopped, him nevermore,
In fragments on the floor,

Him shattered.
Why should he still be here

And not you?
Is that what you wish me to do,

Ghost of my sister?
Or would you let him live?

Would you instead forgive?

CODA: SONG

If you were a song
What song would you be?

Would you be the voice that sings,
Would you be the music?

When I am singing this song for you
You are not empty air

You are here,
One breath and then another:

You are here with me . . .

THE DEAR ONES

But where are they? They can't be nowhere.
It used to be that gypsies took them,
or else the Little People,

who were not little, though enticing.
They were lured into a hill,
those dear ones. There was gold, and dancing.

They should have come home by nine.
You phoned. The clocks chimed
like ice, like metal, heartless.

A week, two weeks: nothing.
Seven years passed. No, a score.
No, a hundred. Make it more.

When they finally reappeared
not a day older
wandering down the road in tatters

in bare feet, their hair all ragged,
those who had waited for them so long
were decades dead.

These were the kinds of stories
we used to tell. They were comforting in a way
because they said

everyone has to be somewhere.
But the dear ones, where are they?
Where? Where? After a while

You sound like a bird.
You stop, but the sorrow goes on calling.
It leaves you and flies out

over the cold night fields,
searching and searching,
over the rivers,
over the emptied air.

They're digging up the Scythians—
the warrior women, the dagger girls,
the hard riders, tattooed up to the armpits
with sinuous animals, and buried with their weapons—

who were not mythical,
who existed after all
(a bracelet, a trinket, a delicate skull),
laid to rest with honour,
them and their axe-felled horses.

They're digging up the arrow maidens
who wandered cityless, then slept unmelted
in the only houses they ever had:
log rooms, log tombs, deep underground.
Frozen for two thousand years,
them and their embroideries,
their silks and leathers, their feathers,

their hacked arm bones, their broken fingers,
their severed heads.
What did you expect? It was war
and they knew what happened if you lost:
rape, death, death, rape,
as brutal as possible, to set a bad example:
babies and young mothers,
girls and boys, all slaughtered.
That's how it went: straight wipeout.
Which is why they fought.
(And for the loot, if victorious.)

Here they are, the nameless ones,
who are still in some way with us.
They knew what happened.
They know what happens.

I missed them again this year.
I was immersed elsewhere
when the weather broke
and enough rain came.

In the treeshade, stealthily,
they nosed up through the sandy loam
and the damp leaf litter—

a sliver of colour, then another—
bringing their cryptic news
of what goes on down there:
the slow dissolve of lignum,
the filaments, the little nodes like fists,
assembling their nets and mists.

Some were bright red, some purple,
some brown, some white, some lemon yellow.
Through the night they nudged,
unfurling like moist fans, living sponges,
like radar dishes, listening.

What did they hear in our human world
of so-called light and air?
What word did they send back down
before they withered?
Was it *Beware*?

Look. The remnants:
a leathery globe of dusty spores,
a nibbled pebbly moon,
a dried half-sphere,
a blackened ear.

Smoke gets in my eyes,
my fifteen eyes.
Glass insulation smoulders.
Pink tongues get stuck on it.
Charred cotton candy.

Did I do that?

Palm tree shorn of its head.
Cathedral ceilings, opened up
to the stars, to the stark.
What did they worship in there?
The overhead fans?
The bolsters? The naked bedspread?

I spy.

They cried *O God* to the pillows.
Now ripped and fluttering,
angel feathers.
These hover, slower than me.
See raw finger paint. Red.
Wet still crawling.

Must have missed something.

Better hone in again.
Do some stuttering.
Attapat. Attatat. Attasis. Attaboom.
Accurate this time. Rah.
Anything saved equals failure.

Was I bad?

Teardrops fall and fall.
The rain shower's broken.

The world's burning up. It always did.
Lightning would strike, the resin
in the conifers explode, the black peat smoulder,
greying bones glow slowly, and the fallen leaves
turn brown and writhe, like paper
held to candle. It's the scent of autumn,
oxidation: you can smell it on your skin,
that sunburn perfume.
                            Only now
it's burning faster. All those yarns
of charred apocalypse concocted
back when we played with matches—
the ardent histories, the Troyish towers
viewed through toppling smoke, the fine
mirage volcanoes that we mimed
with such delight when setting
marshmallows on fire on purpose,

all those slow-fused epics
packed in anthracite, then buried
under granite mountains, or else thrown
into the deepest sea like djinns
in stoneware bottles—

                        All, all are coming true
because we opened the lead seals,
ignored the warning runes,
and let the stories out.
                        We had to know.

We had to know
how such tales really end:
and why.
                        They end in flames
because that's what we want:
we want them to.

In the old days, all werewolves were male.
They burst through their bluejean clothing
as well as their own split skins,
exposed themselves in parks,
howled at the moonshine.
Those things frat boys do.

Went too far with the pigtail-yanking—
growled down into the soft and wriggling
females, who cried *Wee wee*
wee all the way to the bone.
Heck, it was only flirting,
plus a canid sense of fun:
See Jane run!

But now it's different:
No longer gender-specific.
Now it's a global threat.

Long-legged women sprint through ravines
in furry warmups, a pack of kinky
models in sado French *Vogue* getups
and airbrushed short-term memories,
bent on no-penalties rampage.

Look at their red-rimmed paws!
Look at their gnashing eyeballs!
Look at the backlit gauze
of their full-moon subversive halos!
Hairy all over, this belle dame,
and it's not a sweater.

O freedom, freedom and power!
they sing as they lope over bridges,
bums to the wind, ripping out throats
on footpaths, pissing off brokers.

Tomorrow they'll be back
in their middle-management black
and Jimmy Choos
with hours they can't account for
and first dates' blood on the stairs.
They'll make a few calls: *Goodbye.*
It isn't you, it's me. I can't say why.
At sales meetings,
they'll dream of sprouting tails
right in the audiovisuals.
They'll have addictive hangovers
and ruined nails.

Such curious humans, wondering
what song we sang
to lure so many sailors
to their deaths, granted,

but what sort? Of death,
I mean. Sharp birdclaws
in the groin, a rending pain, fanged
teeth in the neck? Or a last breath
exhaled in bliss, like that
of male praying mantises?

I sit here on my frowsy nest
of neckties, quarterly
reports and jockey shorts
mixed in among the bones and pens,
and fluff my breasts and feathers. Lullaby,

my mini-myths, my hungry egglets,
dreaming in your glowing shells
of our failsafe girly secret.
Mama's right nearby
and Daddy must have loved you:
he gave you all his protein!

Hatching's here. Be strong!
Soon I'll hear a tap-tap-tap, Ahoy!
and out you'll break, my babies,
down-covered, rose-toned, lovely
as a pirouette, a lipstick pout,

a candied violet,
flapping your dainty feathery wings
and ravenous with song.

Hour by hour I sign myself—
a smear, a dot, a smear,
white semaphore on the black floor.

Spider shit,
what's left of the enticed:
why is it white?
Because my heart is pure,
though I myself am ulterior,

especially under the bookcase:
a fine place for my silken pockets,
my wisps and filaments,
my looms, my precious cradles.

I've always liked books,
by preference paperbacks,
crumbling and flyspecked.
To their texts I add
my annotations, brash and untidy:

moth wings, beetle husks, my own shed skins
like spindly gloves.
Apt simile: I'm mostly fingers.

I don't like the floor, though.
Too visible, I hunch, I scuttle,
a prey to shoes and vacuums,
not to mention whisks.

If you come across me suddenly
you scream: Too many legs,
or is it the eight red eyes,
the glossy blob of abdomen?
Drop of thumb's blood, popped grape:
that's what you'd aim for.

Though it's bad luck to kill me.
Come to terms:
before you were, I am.
I arrange the rain,
I take harsh care

and while you sleep
I hover, the first grandmother.
I trap your nightmares in my net,
eat the seeds of your fears for you,
suck out their ink

and scribble on your windowsill
these minor glosses on *Is, Is, Is,*
white lullabies.

In our language
we have no words for he or she
or him or her.
It helps if you put a skirt or tie
or some such thing
on the first page.

In the case of a rape, it helps also
to know the age:
a child, an elderly?
So we can set the tone.

We also have no future tense:
what will happen is already happening.
But you can add a word like *tomorrow*
or else *Wednesday*.
We will know what you mean.

These words are for things that can be eaten.
The things that can't be eaten have no words.
Why would you need a name for them?
This applies to plants, birds,
and mushrooms used in curses.

On this side of the table
women do not say No.
There is a word for No, but women do not say it.
It would be too abrupt.
To say No, you can say Perhaps.
You will be understood,
on most occasions.

On that side of the table there are six classes:
unborn, dead, alive,
things you can drink, things you can't drink,
things that cannot be said.

Is it a new word or an old word?
Is it obsolete?
Is it formal or familiar?
How offensive is it? On a scale of one to ten?
Did you make it up?

At the far end of the table
right next to the door,
are those who deal in hazards.
If they translate the wrong word
they might be killed
or at the least imprisoned.
There is no list of such hazards.
They'll find out only after,

when it might not matter to them
about the tie or skirt
or whether they can say No.
In cafés they sit in corners,
backs to the wall.
What will happen is already happening.

Walking in the madman's wood
over the disquieted dry shushing leaves
in early spring.

The madman loved this wildland
once, before his brain
turned lacework. Must have been
him (when?) who put
this round stone here, topping
the mossy oblong. *Mine.*
And all the tin can
lids and wooden squares,
rough-painted red and nailed to trees
to mark his line:
mine, mine, mine, mine.

I shouldn't say that cancelled word:
madman. Maybe *lost his mind?*
No, because we don't have minds
as such these days, but tiny snarls
of firefly neural pathways
signalling *no/yes/no,* suspended
in a greyish cloud
inside a round bone bowl.
Yes: lovely. *No:* too lonely. *Yes.*
The world that we think we see
is only our best guess.

This must have been his shack,
collapsed now, where he'd—what?
Come sometimes and sit? Hepaticas
wrenched up by sun,
brown tufts of hairbrush grass,
the toppled stove, the wild leeks
so glossy they look wet,
the soft log frilled with mushrooms.

You could get waylaid here, or slip amazed
into your tangled head. You could
just not come back.

One by handfuls the feathers fell.
Windsheer, sunbleach, owlwar,
some killer with a shotgun,

who can tell?
But I found them here on the quasi-lawn—
I don't know whose torn skin—

calligraphy of wrecked wings,
remains of a god that melted
too near the moon.

A high flyer once,
as we all were.
Every life is a failure

at the last hour,
the hour of dried blood.
But nothing, we like to think,

is wasted, so I picked up one plume from the slaughter,
sharpened and split the quill,
hunted for ink,

and drew this poem
with you, dead bird.
With your spent flight,

with your fading panic,
with your eye spiralling down,
with your night.

A thrush crashed into my window:
one lovely voice the less
killed by glass as mirror—

a rich magician's illusion of trees—
and by my laziness:
Why didn't I hang the lattice?

Up there in the night air
among the highrises, music dies
as you fire up your fake sunrises:
your light is the birds' last darkness.

All over everywhere
their feathers are falling—
warm, not like snow—
though melting away to nothing.

We are a dying symphony.
No bird knows this,
but us—we know

what our night magic does.
Our dark light magic.

IMPROVISATION ON A FIRST LINE BY YEATS

From *Hound Voice*

Because we love bare hills and stunted trees
we head north when we can,
past taiga, tundra, rocky shoreline, ice.

Where does it come from, this sparse taste
of ours? How long
did we roam this hardscape, learning by heart
all that we used to know:
turn skin fur side in,
partner with wolves, eat fat, hate waste,
carve spirit, respect the snow,
build and guard flame?

Everything once had a soul,
even this clam, this pebble.
Each had a secret name.
Everything listened.
Everything was real,
but didn't always love you.
You needed to take care.

We long to go back there,
or so we like to feel
when it's not too cold.
We long to pay that much attention.
But we've lost the knack;
also there's other music.
All we hear in the wind's plainsong
is the wind.

PLASTICENE SUITE

1. ROCK-LIKE OBJECT ON BEACH

The Paleocene the Eocene
the Miocene the Pleistocene
and now we're here: the Plasticene.

Look, a rock made of sand
and one of lime, and one of quartz,
and one of what is this?

It's black and striped and slippery,
not exactly rock
and not not.

On the beach at any rate.
Petrified oil, with a vein of scarlet,
part of a bucket maybe.

When we're gone and the aliens come
to puzzle out our fossils:
will this be evidence?

Of us: of our too-brief history,
our cleverness, our thoughtlessness,
our sudden death?

2. FAINT HOPES

You could turn it into oil
by cooking it: this has been done.
First you'd have to collect it.
Also there would be a smell.

Some supermarkets have banned it.
Also drinking straws.
Maybe there will be a tax
or other laws.

There are microbes that eat it—
they've been discovered.
But the temperature has to be high:
no good in the North Sea.

You can press it into fake lumber
but only some kinds.
And building blocks, ditto.

You can scoop it out of rivers
before it gets to the sea.
But then what? What do you do with it?

With the overwhelming ongoing
never-ending outpouring?

3. FOLIAGE

"a scrap of black plastic—the defining foliage of the oil age"

MARK COCKER, *OUR PLACE*

It sprouts everywhere, this foliage.
Up in the trees, like mistletoe,
or caught in the marshes

or blooming in the ponds like waterlilies,
gaudy and frilly,
rippling as if alive

or washing onto the beaches, neo-seaweed
of torn bags, cast wrappers, tangled rope
shredded by tides and rocks.

But unlike true foliage it's rootless
and gives nothing back,
not even one empty calorie.

Who plants it, this useless crop?
Who harvests it?
Who can say Stop?

Inside the barebones
ribs it's all bright colour:
a tag a ribbon
a failed balloon
a strip of silver foil
a spring a wheel a coil

What should have been there
inside the sad bag
of wispy feathers
inside the dead bird child?

It should have been the fuel
for wings, it should have been
upsoaring over a clean sea;
not this glittering mess,
this festering nestwork

5. EDITORIAL NOTES

One note might be (she said)
to pull back somewhat
from exhortation and despair

Instead (she said)
try to provide
an experiential under

understanding of human
human (she said) impact
human pact

then let people
let people come
let people come to their own

conclusions.
Own their conclusions.
She said:

There is some danger in this.

You know the old tale:
a machine made by the Devil
that grinds out anything you wish for
with a magic word

and some idiot wishes for salt,
and out comes the salt, more and more,
but he failed to get a handle
on the charm to turn it off

so he throws the thing into the sea,
and that's why the sea is salt.

The Sorcerer's Apprentice—
it's the same story: *Go* is easy,
Stop is the hard part.
In the beginning no one thinks about it.
Then *Wait* is too late.

In our case the sorcerer is dead,
whoever he was to begin with
and we've lost the instructions

and the magic machine grinds on and on
spewing out mountains of whatnot
and we throw it all into the sea
as we have always done
and this will not end well

7. WHALES

Everyone cried when they saw it
in the square blue sea of the TV:
so big and sad

a mother whale
carrying her child
for three days, mourning
its death from toxic plastic.

So big and sad
we can hardly grasp it:
how did we do this by just living
in the normal way,

manoeuvring our way through
package and wrapping,
cutting our way to our food
through the layer by layer that
keeps it fresher,
and doesn't everyone?

What happened before?
How did we ever survive
with only paper and glass and tin
and hemp and leather and oilskin?

But now there's a dead whale
right there on the screen:
so big and sad
something must be done.

It will be! Will it be?
Will we decide to, finally?

This is the little robot
they have just invented
with its cute dollface of soft plastic.
Its expression is confiding
though slightly fearful:
it's designed to learn like a child.

We give it objects:
it fingers them, explores,
it bites and questions,
it plays with them, absorbs.
Then it gets bored
and drops things on the floor.

There might be breakage,
maybe even whimpering.
Does it care?
Have we really gone that far?

It's learning like a child:
how to predict—they tell us—
likely future events:
This will cause that.

Little dollface robot,
what will you make of yourself
in this world we are making?
What will you make of us?

Where will you bestow yourself
when you are obsolete?
On what cosmic trashheap?
Or will you live forever?

Will we become your ancestors,
rapacious and tedious?
Or will you erase us?
Will you drop us on the floor?
Would that be better?

But look on the bright side,
you say.
Has there ever been such brightness?

Has there ever been a flower as bright
that has lasted as long as this?
In winter snow, after a funeral?

Has there ever been a red as red,
a blue as blue?
And so inexpensive too!

Has there ever been a bucket
as light as this, to carry water
into the villages?

Why should we use the heavy one
so easily broken?
Not to mention the orange canoe.

As for your voice, two thousand miles away
but as clear as whistling, right in my ear—
how else could it get here?

Don't tell me this is not beautiful—
as beautiful as the day!
Or some days.

(And the beloved twistable
pea-green always dependable
ice-cube tray . . .)

Pale mauve, pale rose, pale blue,
quirks of the atmosphere:
a bleached Easter.
We gods preside at our own altar.
Hawk face of an old man,
a crone's tyrant jowls.
Lots of jewels.
Offside, lone fisherman in a metal boat
flings away shark parts:
a flurry of beaks and wings.

Lunchtime. Peristalsis of the heart.
Blood squeezed through.
Grit from a lost glacier sifts into our gullets—
grey sand ground from granite—
also limestone: small teeth, fine spines
and midget shells.
They harden us. We open bottles.

Do we have goodwill?
To all mankind?
Not any more.
Did we ever?

When the gods frown, the weather's bad.
When they smile, the sun shines.
We smile all the time now,
smiles of the lobotomized,
and the world fries.

Sorry about that. We got stupid.
We drink martinis and go on cruises.
Whatever we touch turns red.

We pick our way over the slippery rocks
over the stream's foam feathers,
gingerly, in the mist, in the light rain.
Such colours here: crowberries,
round black eyes among the leaves,
red, plum, pink, and orange,
though in a week they'll vanish,
a fact not lost on us.
What's here? A mound of fine white hair?
Has someone been buried?
Yes, many, over the years,
though this is only lichen.

Here are the ravens, as if on cue.
Will you be next? they ask us.
They understand waned flesh:
so eager for a beakful.
Wait a little, we say to them.
Everything in good time.
Meanwhile the ponds are beautiful,
the yellow stones, green moss, the scurvy grass,
the long-abandoned graves, the small old willows.

My truelove limps along the street
hayfoot strawfoot lame foot
who once was an army marcher.

He's up there now, ahead, in silhouette
against bright windows, against
the leather coats, the Sunglass Hut,
the Ladies' Jewellery:

Hayfoot, straw . . .
Now gone. Blended with shadow.

Maybe not himself. Not the same one,
the strider in the autumn woods, leaves yellow,
a whiff of snow
on the frozen ground, bears around,
a skim of ice on the pond,
then uphill, hayfoot, me gasping
to keep up.

What happened? What became?
Why are you still walking?
said the doctor. You have no knee.
Yet on he limps, unseen by me
behind the corner,
willing himself to get there:
to some warm haven, kindly nook
or drink, or chair.

The red light changes. Darkness clots:
it's him all right,
not even late, his cane foot
hayfoot, straw,
slow march. It's once

it's once upon
a time, it's cane
as tic, as tock.

MR. LIONHEART

Mr. Lionheart is away today.
He comes and goes,
he flickers on and off.
You might have heard a roar,
you might not.

What is it he forgot
this last time?
I don't mean the keys, the hat.
I mean his tawny days,
the sun, the golden running.
All of our furry dancing.
It returns to him in flashes,

but then what? Then regret
because we're not.
There's birdsong, however,
from birds whose names have vanished.

Birds don't need them, those lost names.
We needed them, but that was then.
Now, who cares?
Lions don't know they are lions.
They don't know how brave they are.

It was a problem in comic books:
drawing an invisible man.
They'd solve it with a dotted line
that no one but us could see,

us with our snub noses pressed to the paper,
the invisible glass between us and the place
where invisible men can exist.

That's who is waiting for me:
an invisible man
defined by a dotted line:

the shape of an absence
in your place at the table,
sitting across from me,
eating toast and eggs as usual
or walking ahead up the drive,
a rustling of the fallen leaves,
a slight thickening of the air.

It's you in the future,
we both know that.
You'll be here but not here,
a muscle memory, like hanging a hat
on a hook that's not there any longer.

SILVER SLIPPERS

No dancing any more, but still
wearing my silver shoes

my silver slippers,
all of their wishes used up

and no way to get home.
I'll skip dinner, the kind with linens

and candles lit for two. I'll be alone,
sitting across from an absence.

Oh where did you go, and when?
It wasn't to Kansas.

I'll perch in this hotel room solo
and nibble a square of cheddar

saved up from the plane.
Also the salted almonds.

These will tide me over.
I won't be hungry.

I'll act as if I am busy.
But none of this will defend me:

not the silken bedsheets
the pillows ballooning aloft,

not even the happiness travel mag
with its conjuror's dreams—

the winged monkey brain
flying me to neverland,

such coziness and shelter—
those don't make up for it.

It, the moment we know is coming,
the click of the seconds

on the skyblue bedside alarm,
countdown as the flying house descends

to silent crash, dead witchy heart
plus empty silver shoes, end stop.

WITHIN

Outside we see a shrivelling,
but from within, as felt
by heart and breath and inner skin, how different,
how vast   how calm   how part of everything
how starry dark. Last breath. Divine
perhaps. Perhaps relief. The lovers caught
and sealed inside a cavern,
voices raised in one last hovering
duet, until the small wax light
goes out. Well anyway
I held your hand and maybe
you held mine
as the stone or universe closed in
around you.
Though not me. I'm still outside.

It's an old word, fading now.
Dearly did I wish.
Dearly did I long for.
I loved him dearly.

I make my way along the sidewalk
mindfully, because of my wrecked knees
about which I give less of a shit
than you may imagine
since there are other things, more important—
wait for it, you'll see—

bearing half a coffee
in a paper cup with—
dearly do I regret it—
a plastic lid—
trying to remember what words once meant.

Dearly.
How was it used?
Dearly beloved.
Dearly beloved, we are gathered.
Dearly beloved, we are gathered here
in this forgotten photo album
I came across recently.

Fading now,
the sepias, the black and whites, the colour prints,
everyone so much younger.
The Polaroids.
What is a Polaroid? asks the newborn.
Newborn a decade ago.

How to explain?
You took the picture and then it came out the top.

The top of what?
It's that baffled look I see a lot.
So hard to describe
the smallest details of how—
all these dearly gathered together—
of how we used to live.
We wrapped up garbage
in newspaper tied with string.
What is newspaper?
You see what I mean.

String though, we still have string.
It links things together.
A string of pearls.
That's what they would say.
How to keep track of the days?
Each one shining, each one alone,
each one then gone.
I've kept some of them in a drawer on paper,
those days, fading now.
Beads can be used for counting.
As in rosaries.
But I don't like stones around my neck.

Along this street there are many flowers,
fading now because it is August
and dusty, and heading into fall.
Soon the chrysanthemums will bloom,
flowers of the dead, in France.
Don't think this is morbid.
It's just reality.

So hard to describe the smallest details of flowers.
This is a stamen, nothing to do with men.
This is a pistil, nothing to do with guns.
It's the smallest details that foil translators
and myself too, trying to describe.
See what I mean.

You can wander away. You can get lost.
Words can do that.

Dearly beloved, gathered here together
in this closed drawer,
fading now, I miss you.
I miss the missing, those who left earlier.
I miss even those who are still here.
I miss you all dearly.
Dearly do I sorrow for you.

Sorrow: that's another word
you don't hear much any more.
I sorrow dearly.

In the early morning an old woman
is picking blackberries in the shade.
It will be too hot later
but right now there's dew.

Some berries fall: those are for squirrels.
Some are unripe, reserved for bears.
Some go into the metal bowl.
Those are for you, so you may taste them
just for a moment.
That's good times: one little sweetness
after another, then quickly gone.

Once, this old woman
I'm conjuring up for you
would have been my grandmother.
Today it's me.
Years from now it might be you,
if you're quite lucky.

The hands reaching in
among the leaves and spines
were once my mother's.
I've passed them on.
Decades ahead, you'll study your own
temporary hands, and you'll remember.
Don't cry, this is what happens.

Look! The steel bowl
is almost full. Enough for all of us.

The blackberries gleam like glass,
like the glass ornaments
we hang on trees in December
to remind ourselves to be grateful for snow.

Some berries occur in sun,
but they are smaller.
It's as I always told you:
the best ones grow in shadow.

UNCOLLECTED

POEMS II

(1991–2023)

✦ ✦ ✦

How far we have come
in our boat of paper!
At first it was only a word
scrawled in the sand by a small child.

Then all at once it had a sail
and very soon, a motor,
a plot propelled by air,
the steel blades slicing through time.

Look how fast we were going!
Boat after paper
boat, what a good idea!
Sailing us anywhere!

And that's where we went, for a while.
Basking and suntans were ours.
You could see so far down.
Such divine swimming!

Though, oops, there were no more beach houses.
It made for a cleaner look.
That was the plus. *Adjustment,* we said.
We got used to the limited salads

and those faux nut things, what were their names?
By now there were too many
paper boats. They were setting fires
and eating things we won't mention.

This is not for us, we said.
Let's head for the ramparts
whatever they may be,
where a person can feel secure

and we can have a decent shower,
get rid of that smell
which does tend to seep in everywhere.
By then all the cats had gone missing.

However. On, on, we sang. No matter what
we've got the spirit
written all over our boat:
with it, we can corner the future!

Tomorrow will be whatever
you dream, we said as we rocked to sleep
on our paper boat that by now was flying.
We're almost there! Hear the cheering?

Now here, in this morning, we're stranded.
Crap, we say. What happened?
There's nothing here but sand
and a small child scratching on it

with a stick: *And, and, and, and, and*

AH PEOPLE

Ah people. A trail of burnt-out
campfires where we once gnawed roots and thighbones
and sang songs we thought could well accomplish
something. More hooves and antlers. Food for the winter.

The place where we entered each other
marked by the standing stones the moon rose
behind, making the ebb
and flow of blood, and we worshipped
something through each other, who knows
what? So many languages
forgotten, junked
in these middens, along with
the goat skulls. Blue beads. Worn-out skins
of foxes. Throat-slit sons. Charms
for good weather. Infant daughters.

Left there while we moved on,
carrying the fires . . .

I want this to be a small book,
a small, slight book, easy to carry,
the sort of book you would tuck in at the last minute
to read on a plane

to read on a plane you yourself took out of impulse,
a melancholy impulse, with rage in it as well.
You will take this plane, but you may not take it back.

Let them wonder. Let that one person wonder. This would be just,
considering all the love you have failed to receive.
Meanwhile you are walking alone under strange palm trees,

sneered at by the locals, you and your thin-skinned feet
and your peeling nose and rancorous thoughts,
and you've forgotten the book, in the airplane magazine pocket.

I want this to be the kind of book a man might find
as he cleans the last airplane you have ever taken.
He sees the book and hesitates: should he throw it out?

But no, he can tell: this book was left there just for him.
Perhaps it was written just for him. He has despaired
of such a thing ever happening, so much so

that he's almost given up reading, and slumps in a stupor in front
of the television instead. But now here is this book,
his book, and he snatches at it as if stealing,

and hides it under his shirt, and takes it home,
because this is the sort of book that passes itself
from hand to hand, unnoticed by most, like a microbe.

The room he takes it to is not a room with books.
This is the only one. It sits there now
on his kitchen table, beside the dried remains

of the scrambled eggs he had for breakfast, and he looks at it.
He's almost afraid to open it. What will it say?
It will say what it has always said: his name,

or yours, because by now it's you,
it is you reading this message, which is a cry
for help, the silent cry you sent out when you got on the plane.

This book has you by heart. It knows you backwards,
you and your sulky anguish, because you're in it
now, you're in this book,
it's reading you, you're caught by it, you can't get out.

EFFIGY OF A POET, IN A PARK

For Al Purdy

You hear what they're saying, the young ones
as they sit on your plinth, legs newly bare,
self-medicating on warped puns
or weeping into their notebooks:
the plaints, the sadness, the rages,
the longing, the wrenching despair.

But why? you wonder.
Why such lament?
Oh, right. They're still tethered
to their bodies, mired
in that long flesh song, that enchantment.

Can you remember it,
that singing in chains?
That craziness of spring?
Yes, you say. More or less.
It's like hearing a jazz parade
streets off: the drum throb, the wailing,
the sax, the sex.

Not coming this way. Growing fainter
while you, now a statue,
birds on your hands and head,
unshackled from the weighty imagery
that once enthralled you,
emptied of pain
and of everything you ever said,

gaze at an angle
out of your stone eyes
up at the leaves
looking undead but wise,
while also, up there in the sky . . .

What then?
Make an effort.
Finish the thought.
But why?
But why not?

THREE-EYES

For Phyllis Webb; after the Brothers Grimm

The three-eyed sister bumps into doors
because she's looking through them.
These are her bruises,
these blue shadows under her two
other eyes, the ones that close.

Three-eyes sees the slow turmoil
in the interiors of stones,
the grey light thrown out by shadows.
When she walks in the green spring wood,
her feet shrivel in the fire
that will burn there fifty years later.
For her, the clean cities disclose their hidden
plagues, their sores, their greasy sewers,
and lovers unfold their looming
dreams of murder.

You rent her sight
when you need a piece
of hard truth or a slice of the future,
but you would not want to be her.
This festival of paper
cups and hips, this kiss
that made you so happy:
this is not her party.

She could have had two eyes, like you.
She could have learned to dance
and snared a prince.
She could have had an amputation,
but made her choice.

Look into this well
in which many have drowned,
and you will see water
or your own reflection,
your own plausible smile.
The three-eyed sister sees further.
She sees into you,
right down to the bone.

OLD LETTERS DISCOVERED

For Gwen MacEwen

Here they are again,
as immediate as when we wrote.
Your envelopes with the red sealing wax
or the Egyptian eyes,
your deliberately zany letters,
my more than sane replies.

I've been sewing clothes when drunk, you wrote.
Have you ever done that?
A question I ignored, among others.

Desperate play. Edged signals.

You liked walking the ledges, outside the window,
fifty storeys up, at midnight.
You liked looking down
while one of your other voices told you to jump
because it might be flying,
and the third one held your hand.
Those who are so alone soon multiply.

When you wrote, I was always away somewhere,
as you were. In the same city
we scarcely saw each other.

The people we knew were alive then.
Now most of them aren't, you included.

Dead means you'll never say anything more.
But also, in your case,
you'll never say anything less.

ANOTHER JOAN OF ARC POEM

Or think of her as glass,
a sheer thin sphere of it,
a hardened bubble

confided to the sea
how many centuries ago
and washed up here

on this dilapidated shore
among the plastic bags
and salty rope

a charmed bottle
carrying a message
you can see in there

on a wisp of paper,
each letter clear,
each word illegible.

Now that our tasty liaison is over,
the monster slaughtered, the palace going under,
the black-draped ships embarked,
and I'm stuck on this feckless
island with a dipsomaniac
in lion skins, and you've sailed off to do in your father
and pretend it was an accident, like the hypocrite you are

I might as well tell you: the minotaur
was my friend. Or not friend. More
like an associate. I'd go in there
through the labyrinth, which I knew
in the dark, luckily,
because it was always dark,
holding on to my silver thread,
and consult him about things.

What things? you wonder.
You know—the future,
the deaths of kings, the meanings
of snakeskins and birds' intestines.
His answers were exact,
Though muffled.

In return I brought him morsels. Youths with edged weapons
and grandiose plans, like you.
I stood at the far side of the room,
steering clear of the horns.
He could get out of hand
and was prone to tantrums.

In the food fights, he always won,
and would have won
against you too, if I hadn't cheated.
I spiked the wine, what else?

I thought I was trading
prophecy for love. Bad choice.
But I've got news for you:
You've made a bad choice too.

Nothing but baritones will do.
I've had it with tenors.
I no longer want to climb the stairs
in the company of well-pressed men
with tonsils, nifty swords,
neat boots, thin noses,
their chests festooned with gold
braid, gold chains, and necklaces
of previous women's teeth.

I've done the balconies,
nights on the heights, head notes, flute solos,
the chandelier-shattering arias,
the lutes, the budded roses:
that's only fun in white nightgowns.

Now I want cellars.
Down there, where the beet wine's kept,
the sandbound potatoes,
the old honey, the cellos,
the umbers, ochre tones,
the thrown-out bric-a-brac,
the shambles.

What I have in mind
is something once earthen,
rumpled, fattish, mournful,
hair-covered and dark.
A bitter chocolate melancholy,
not wolf but bear,
reproachful, clumsy, grateful,
trained by hunger.

It's the base note I want.
If there's trouble, it won't be
because he's taken us up too high
but down too low.

There was a mistake at his birth,
a baleful star:
otherwise he would have been a tenor.

This is what he thinks,
regarding himself in full costume
via the backstage mirror.

He's condemned to black and silver,
purple at the very most.
No gold, no yellow.
It's so unfair.

Objectively, he's not repulsive.
He's just as handsome as the other fellow.
Better: he's not fat.

He has a white smile,
his canine teeth no longer than normal:
they only seem that way.
He looks fine in a slouchy hat.

But to suffer, over and over—
such disdain! Such rejection!
It's more than any man should bear.

Whenever he makes his entrance—
he aims for a leonine saunter—
the soprano faints, or freezes,
or throws up high shrieks.

He has so much to give her!
She's eaten his heart
with her corrosive music.
His love is poisonous dust.

Therefore he must practise gloating,
and grimacing with unchaste lust,
and varieties of bad laughter
in the caves of the lower registers,
and the twisted postures of despair.

THIRTY

I stand with my mouth ajar while one girl
who is thirty-three tells another
who has just made it to thirty
that thirty will be okay.
There's a knack to it, she says, because
thirty is when you say
I am who I am. This is it.

Do you ever reach a point at which
you don't find the children hilarious?
By children, I mean—you understand—
anyone younger than you.

Just wait till forty, I think.
Forty is when you say, Hey, wait,
I am not who I am!
Let's go over this again!

After that, there's a few more surprises,
If you get that far—
that far into the woods
you keep hoping you're out of.

We slowly morph into revisionists.
That cold bright ardour,
that absolute truth of the firing squad
goes to the wall.
We lose interest in being right,
also in killing.
We can't even kill our previous selves.
It's pardons all round.

1.

Newsstands blow up
for no reason. Bookstores as well.
You're clamped to a windowsill
gibbering with adrenalin
as the light-beam swings past you.
Holy hell, you whisper.
Those words are finally meaningful.

2.

The woman you were certain loved you
did not. Never did.
A puckered heart she had,
testicle on a plate
three days cold.
She used to cut your grapefruit for you,
have a Scotch waiting,
knives and poisons on her mind.
Now she's got sunglasses.
Who seduced her?

3.

Those girls manacled to the wall—
you laughed at them in old movies.
They used to wear torn jumpsuits.
You thought they were a prop.
But now they're everywhere,
naked from the waist down,
pink, black, bruise purple.

4.

Too many cars ruined,
festooned with red and grey.
Vein glue, brain jelly
all over the upholstery.
They'll never get the smell out,
whoever cleans up afterwards.
It's an art.
Nobody sees that part.

5.

That older man in the suit,
the one with the briefcase,
the sneering one, with the shaved head—
you've seen him before.
Your stern, mean father
come back from the dead,
his neck a snarl of sutures.
He says, *I told you not to.*
How waterproof are you?

6.

Everything's suddenly clearer,
though also more obscure.
You don't have to love anyone.
That eon's over.
But how free you feel!
How buoyant, as you're floating
from rooftop to rooftop,
leaking time from your many punctures
as the Glocks tick and tock.

7.

Behind you there's howling.
Ahead, an unturned corner.
There's fur on your nape. There's fear.
Wake up! Wake up!
In all these dreams, you're falling.

WATCHMAN

In the fading light
you stand at the gate
you watch.
They go out, they come in,
they don't see you.
It's more dangerous at night.

Someone has to watch.
That is the way with castles,
with fortresses, however new.
You are invisible
despite all that leather

Nothing keeps happening.
They come in, they go out.
To them you are a blur.
You are dispensable

until there is a shot or shout,
and something keeps happening.
You throw yourself in front
of the ones who don't see you.

Something stops happening.
You lie at the gate.
There are feet at eye level.
You watch the feet in their fading shoes
in the fading light.

The gods like the old songs
because they know them.
Hum a few bars for them
and the words come back,

at least the choruses.
The one about the man
who ate his children,
they'll dance to that.

The one about the woman
who married her own son
and hanged herself, and he was blinded:
they set that up.

Serves her right
for not killing her doomed baby,
and if she had, the payback
would have served her right as well.

They like the songs about slipping into
animal bodies, such as bulls and swans—
better sex that way,
with death woven in—
dirtying themselves with mortals.
Those were the days!

They like the old songs.
Older than old. The hymns
of human sacrifice.
Blood on the altar.
Now that was glory,
the fumes of burning flesh
ascending like incense.
Now we're getting serious.

They like that song the best.
It's the reddest.
They're still playing it,
they play it over and over.

It sounds like a stormy seashore,
It sounds like the roar
of a thousand voices.
It sounds like mothers howling.
It sounds like war.

—

THE DISASTERS OF WAR: A SEQUEL

What is your wish, my child?
From me and the magic hat,
the magic lamp, the magic stick,
the trick, the shoes, whatever:
A dress? A prince? A horse?

I want him back.

What do you mean by *him*?

Him. The one he was
before he went away.
How sweet he was on that day
we drifted out in the green canoe
and he said he'd love me forever.

Your wish violates the borders.
There are two kinds of wounds:
the visible, the invisible,
and of those, two kinds,
wounds inflicted and wounds received.
All are lethal.

The one you loved is gone.
Shards of him scattered here and there.
You must love this other,
though he's an imposter.
This love will wear you down.
Damaged people damage people,
and so on.

But can't you only—what he said?

There's no forever,
not on this side of the river.

I could give you a box of hope, instead—
people seem to like it—

Or else these pictures.
They tell what he saw.
Many have travelled far
to the place of fire and blackout,
the time without words.
Some have survived,
though not intact.
No one comes back.

Things are muddier than we were led to expect.
Not worse as such, just muddier.
No bedrock ledge, no granite.

There are maps but no map.
There are many estuaries
but which one hides the enemies?

Which enemies?
That too is muddier.
Their gas masks are so blurred.

These are my orders:
Go steadily forward,
crouching perhaps, perhaps running,

taking advantage of bushes.
I did not mean that sexually,
whoever sniggered.

There are reeds, there are rushes,
there are fens and sedges.
Our feet are already bleached,

we brought the wrong footgear.
This will be the buddy system:
handcuff yourselves to your partners,

stay close, hold tight, don't let them slither,
even when they melt
around the edges, or moult,

the skin cracking
right down the back,
but never fear!

I'll get you out alive!
Or was that last year?
As I said, things are muddier.

We've been here before.

MY GRADE FIVE CLASS RECITING "IN FLANDERS FIELDS,"
REMEMBRANCE DAY

The echoes last so long.
Seventy-odd years on
the chorus continued to intone.

It was always a ghost story.
The dead were speaking
through our nine-year-old mouths,

line by fumbled line, reciting
the fields of blood-red poppies,
the singing larks, the guns,

the shattered faces, telling
how their once-living hearts
had bled and also loved,

and how their hands had failed.
(But what about the torch?
What was it? And why passed?)

Do not break faith, they whispered,
and we promised. (But why died?
But faith in what?)

Not *in* but *with,* they said.
Faith with us, unsleeping.
Do not break.

Learn it by heart, they said.
So we did.

Grey drops of melancholy pock the air
like rain on a pond, like asteroids
on a molten moon:
impact, then ripple spreading out
from the epicentre of sadness.

Where does it come from, all this gloom?
Is someone somewhere happy?

They must be, or we'd blur into a twilight
uniform as cold porridge
in which all dogs are fog,
but reading poetry you wouldn't know it:
such tasteful misery.

What happened to the Muse of Fire
with her flame-red wings, her ecstasy,
her whirling dancers—
what extinguished her?

Here comes the Muse of Sorrow,
grey, as I told you; a damp visitor
slipping in over the lintel.

Farewell, she says. (Bell tolling
in the background.) Nevermore.
Her face of bone reflects yours,
a glass door.

Try it this way:
I'm trapped in a cave
or it might be a stone tower.
Echoes. The drip of water.

Possibly there's a skylight:
Some form of illumination,
Say a torch or flare.

Given that, I can scratch on the wall
or the lintel, or the rim of a well.
My name, perhaps. The year.
Some rudimentary graffiti:

Here lie I, a poor prisoner—
That sort of thing.
I won't get out: that's not the point.

What is, then? The point?
Passing the time?
Leaving a trace of myself
for someone to find later?
Some hapless reader.

I was here, once,
inside this cave or tower
where you are standing now.
It took me a week, inscribing
with a nail, a shard, a file,
this word on stone for you:

RESISTER.

Tell me something good,
just one good thing, just tell me
something that will get me through
the hours the days the weeks that bring
nothing of any goodness, just more
news of other things like
spoiled meat or else raw
bones the dogs keep dragging in from god
knows where, what bombed-out car or ocean
wreck, whose child's ribs wrenched
open, what woman's torso torn like
bread, whose sons now head-
less, what trashed home, what
oily sludge a hundred miles
wide on which we feed, the words pour in, the door
won't close. O stop, go mute,
just one good thing instead is all I ask.
So let's say *green*
buds. Or wait, there aren't a lot of those, just one
green bud might do, despite.
No. Wait. Let's say a person said
Hello, and not unkindly. No. Let's say
that it got cooler, or else warmer, or the rain
finished, or else it rained, whichever one
was needed. No. Instead say *breakfast.*
That could do it.
A faint shimmering
of plates and pearly spoons, a tender cup, what comfort!
There. That's thirty minutes passed, at any
rate. The gate defended
for a little space, and wasn't that
enough? No. Wait.

PYJAMAS WITH SHEEP ON THEM

These PJs have a strange device:
mauve sheep, smiling, eyes closed.
Also, writing—*Sleepy Sheep*—
on flannel.
How cozy. How adorable.

Someone gave these to me,
their idea—presumably—
of who I have become:
fuzzy and huggable as a pillow,
round and babyish, or very old—
whatever age the adult middle ground
is not.
This happens when you're short.

Maybe though like real sheep:
smelly and stupid.
Anyway, asleep. Thus harmless,
tucked into a safe space.

That isn't what I come upon
down in the night world, though.
Instead, precipices.
Mazes and escapes. Remorse, and words
that were not said.
Encounters with the dead,
who turn away from me, still angry.

(Did I find brightness? Maybe.
Meadows? Flowered pastures?
Greetings? Glad surprises?)

(My dearest, is it you?)

BAD HEART

Heart, you nitwit—
taking off like a stray dog
skittering on the highway
in a panic, then freezing
seconds away from a crash—

Get back in here! Sit down!
No need to jump around!

Bad Heart pays no attention.
It's locked in its ribcage now,
rebellious, growling.

It wants to fool around,
knock, sing, and shout.
It wants to be free of me.
It wants out.

SCATTERING WOOD

This is the scattering wood
where we are scattered:
ashes, broken teeth,
the afterlife of smoke.

Who was I when you were
who you were? Who were you?
Among the trees is traditional
for the lost and wandering, so I go in.

Tidy mourners have been here,
ringing the trunks of maples
with powdery burned circlets.
Others, less thoughtful,
have left their flowers to wither,
potted chrysanthemums mostly,
with tinsel and leached ribbons.
Some place round stones.

It's half-light under the leaves,
tints of grey and silver;
the kinds of plants you'd expect—
nightshade, some kind of creeper;

not much of a forest,
you can't go deeper in.
But still, time vanishes
and you feel your skin
already turning to mist.

Where have you gone? If anywhere,
dear ones and twos and threes,
let's hope it isn't here.

IN PAIN

Pleasure, it seems, does not have walls,
is not an attic, cellar,
well, tunnel, or other container:
nothing you can get stuck in,
unlike pain.

But if pain's an edifice,
important to know what kind:
The flophouse of pain? The tacky bungalow
of pain? Heartbreak Hotel?
The Paingate Luxury Condos?

No, more like a jail,
though even jails have openings.
In theory, there's always an exit,
if only through a sheerfall doorway.
At least he's no longer in pain,

they say, as if that's consoling.
But look: across the fence
and in the unbound meadow, is there?
A trace? A glimmering
shadow? A white horse, running?

Pickerel weed in bloom.
In the shadows of what was once
our garden, annuals battle the weeds.

Puffballs like tiny rubber bubbles
drift up through sandy darkness.
I dreamed this once.

I'm wearing the same shirt
I wore here that year,
that year we gave up our standoffs
and skirmishes, and took up tenderness.

Barring some crisis,
our clothing will outlive us.
None of which we mentioned
while holding hands on the dock

at duskfall, as the darkness
bloomed in us, though not
like flowers, and daytime
shut itself down.

Who knows its name, this darkness?
It's merely there, a condition
for stars. We did not say,
Everything's winding down.

We've been very lucky,
we said instead.

The green thing, the yellow thing, the brown thing,
the dull red thing in the upside-down bottle,
the bottles, the jars, the colourful tubes
handcrafted with care, they say:
chilled archaeology.

The tiny print that codes Best Before:
but all those Best dates are far in the past,
back when you were still walking,
still sleeping, still waking, still daily.

Why didn't I do this earlier?
Why are these jars still here?
They're full of old time, green, brown, and yellow
and red, long overdue for the tossout:

time going stale, time growing
tiny grey spores, tiny poisons.
No more feasts this year.
What are they for,

these little jars of sadness,
these jars of tears?

Was this the best I could do—
soup from a can, egg in a cup,
the heel of last week's bread?

What happened to our old largesse,
abundance, plenitude,
our garden overflow, our flavours
honed and shining?

You forgot about knives and flames,
which dial, which button,
which clove or onion.

I tried to improvise
but was bad at it.
I'd lost the flair.

I set down my offering—
some kind of clam chowder
with frozen peas added—
pretending all was as usual.

But this is wonderful! you said
In the evening sunlight.
Thank you. Thank you for making it.

I love you now, right now
inside this one word *now,* the one you're reading
now. And then of course this means
I love you now forever, just as
long as you can stay inside
this lemon egg of time
your mouth makes as
you say this word—now try it—see,
an egg of air,
and you will be protected now by
such a soft round sound
though now, just now,
the loose assemblage of the sounds
I think of now as *I*
may now have long since drifted
softly into the air, I'm dustmotes now, but just
start over, start up there
again, just where I say I love
you now, right
now right

ACKNOWLEDGEMENTS

Paper Boat is a selection from the first moment my poems appeared in book form until now.

Nobody pushes a huge boulder up a hill alone, and thinking you could be a writer, in the Canada of the late 1950s and early 1960s, was a huge boulder. In fact, so sparse did the literary territory seem then that any older writer advising you—supposing you might encounter one—told you that if you wanted to be a writer you should move to New York or London or Paris, where such a wish might be understood, and where the physical means—such as publishing companies open to new writers—might actually exist.

I began as a writer during this arid period, continued during the reinvention of Canadian publishing, and benefited from the changes that occurred during the 1960s and 1970s, including the advent of public readings and the arrival of second-wave feminism. A great many people along the way encouraged, edited, and published these poems. Others helped with business and life tasks, thus freeing time for me to write. Not all of these people are still alive—the stash of those my age or older is rapidly shrinking—but I will thank them anyway, in the order of their appearance in my life.

1950S TO 1966

Thanks to: My high-school English teacher Bessie Billings, who said of one of my juvenile poems, "I don't understand this at all, dear, so it must be good." My aunt Joyce Killam Barkhouse, who when I was an undergraduate sent an early poem to Lindsay Bennett of Dalhousie, who in turn sent it to Douglas Lochhead, an actual poet, who said I had talent and should be encouraged. Jay Macpherson, fellow poet and professor of Victorian literature at Victoria College in the University of Toronto. Gail Youngberg McConnell, editor of *Acta*

Victoriana, the college literary magazine, where I published a lot of things in 1959–61; Dennis Lee, fellow student and fellow poet, who comes into the story later. Also John Robert Colombo, who curated the poetry evenings at the Bohemian Embassy coffeehouse, founded by Don Cullen and located up a flight of stairs in an exposed-brick warehouse type of building. It showcased jazz and folk singing, and had a poetry night on Thursdays; I did my first rather bad public readings there, circa 1960–61. There was a short-lived purple mimeo magazine that came out of these readings: it was called *The Sheet.* At this time I also read A.J.M. Smith's anthology of Canadian poetry and the *Oxford Book of Canadian Verse* in English.

I thank Gwendolyn MacEwen, fellow poet. John Colombo also owned the small flatbed press on which fellow poet David Donnell and I handset *Double Persephone* (1961), selections from which are the first things you will read in this book. This was a suite of seven poems, with a cover printed by linoblock, in an edition of under two hundred copies. It sold for fifty cents, worth more at the time than it is now, but still not very much money. I wish I'd kept a few more.

I thank also a number of literary magazine editors of the time, including Milton Wilson (*Canadian Forum*), Robert Weaver (*Tamarack Review* and the producer of the CBC Radio program *Anthology*), and poet and dramatist James Reaney (*Alphabet* magazine).

I thank John Robert Colombo (again) and Jacques Godbout, editors of *Poésie/Poetry 64,* a bilingual anthology of young Canadian poets—published just before the Separatist movement got going, and possibly the last moment at which a Québecois poet might feel comfortable in a book with the word *Canadian* on the cover.

I thank Charles Pachter, longtime friend and collaborator, whose first handmade and illustrated book was the suite of poems called "The Circle Game."

I thank Raymond Souster, Peter Miller, and Louis Dudek, whose Contact Press published my first full-length collection, also called *The Circle Game,* in 1966. I did the cover using Letraset for the type and stick-on red legal dots for the spiral design. (It was cheaper than having a designer do it.) Having unexpectedly won Canada's only big literary prize at that time, the Governor General's Award, and having been already out of print by that time—Contact Press editions were small—this book was reprinted in 1967 by the House of Anansi Press, newly founded by David Godfrey and my college friend Dennis Lee.

The late 1960s saw an expansion of public poetry readings—from the small and crowded Bohemian Embassy to larger events at universities and evenings at bookstores and in high-school gymnasiums and old movie theatres. I did quite a lot of this kind of thing in the late 1960s and into the 1970s and 1980s, and indeed over the next thirty years, though the emphasis shifted from poetry to fiction to onstage conversations, all of which were followed by book signings.

Due to my various travels in the late 1960s and early 1970s, I met other poets and writers across Canada, including many who remained friends throughout our lives. I mention only a few: Al Purdy, P.K. Page, D.G. Jones, John Newlove, bill bissett, George Bowering, Matt Cohen (whom I edited at Anansi), Roy Kiyooka, Michael Ondaatje, Alice Munro, Marian Engel, Audrey Thomas, and Jane Rule and Helen Sonthoff. Dear Readers.

1968–1980

William Toye of Oxford University Press, Canada, came into my life with *The Animals in That Country* (1968). He was then a young and enthusiastic editor, "one of the first people to usher in an expanded and flourishing Canadian publishing business," says Wikipedia. At that time, Oxford Canada published perhaps two books of poetry a year, so I was thrilled. With Bill, I went on to publish *The Journals of Susanna Moodie* (1970), creating also the cover and a set of collages made up of period prints and watercolour illustrations. (This book later appeared as a spectacularly illustrated and very large serigraph edition by Charles Pachter, which was later made available as a reproduction edition.)

Thanks to my first husband, James Polk, one-time fellow student and fellow writer, always very supportive of my poetry.

Susanna Moodie was followed by *Procedures for Underground*, first published in 1970 by Little, Brown, the editor being Peter Davison. At the same time, I published the long suite of somewhat ferocious poems, *Power Politics* (1971), with the House of Anansi Press, the editor being Dennis Lee. In that year I also (briefly) took over the poetry list at Anansi.

Two more books with Oxford, Bill Toye being editor, followed in the 1970s: *You Are Happy* (1974) and *Selected Poems* (1976). There was a U.S. edition of the latter volume by Simon & Schuster. *Two-Headed Poems* (1978), again with Oxford. In the United States, the editor was Fran McCullough, then with Harper & Row. This publication was facilitated by Phoebe Larmore, who became my agent in 1971, continued so for over forty years, and remains a dear friend and Dear Reader.

In the 1970s, poetry—the dominant form in Canada during the 1960s, partly because publishers were reluctant to take on the expense of a novel unless they could get a U.S. or a U.K. or a French co-publisher—began to diminish in relative importance as prose fiction took centre stage. However, during the 1970s I continued to publish in various magazines. I'll mention Stuart Friebert of Oberlin and *FIELD* magazine as a constant supporter, as well as George Hitchcock of *Kayak* magazine and Joyce Carol Oates of the *Ontario Review*. Also Robin Skelton of *The Malahat Review* and Karen Mulhallan of *Descant*. Who have I left out? Many, I'm sure. I'm also sure I'll hear about it.

In the 1980s, *True Stories* came out in 1981—the cover was a watercolour I did—and *Interlunar* in 1984, again with a cover of a watercolour. *Selected Poems II* appeared in 1986.

Nan Talese, then of Houghton Mifflin, was now my American editor—she had published *The Handmaid's Tale*—and she brought out *Selected Poems* and *Selected Poems II*.

Bill Toye retired in 1991, and the age of poetry at Oxford Canada—or at least my relationship with it—came to an end. At McClelland & Stewart, long the publisher of my fiction in Canada under various editors, Ellen Seligman was now my editor, and she published my next poetry book, *Morning in the Burned House* (1995). My father had died in 1993, and a number of the poems are about him. I'd had a long relationship with Virago in the U.K., where Lennie Goodings, who'd been on my first book tour in the U.K. (and we will repress that meal in Manchester), was now the editorial director. She brought out a U.K. Selected, *Eating Fire,* in 1998. My U.K. agent of the time, Vivienne Schuster of Curtis Brown, helped arrange this, and remains a dear friend.

The next collection was *The Door* (2007), with Ellen Seligman as Canadian editor and Lennie Goodings at Virago in the U.K, and a U.S. edition by Houghton Mifflin. I did the cover: this time I hand-coloured and scratched a photo of myself on my eighth birthday, standing in front of (what else) a door. My sleeves are too short, as are my pantlegs—we'd been in the woods until early November, with no chance to buy anything that fit. I look forlorn—like an orphan—and indeed by the time I'd created the cover I was one, as my mother had died in 2006.

I continued to write poems over the next twelve years, but did not publish them until 2020, the year after Graeme Gibson, my partner of forty-eight years, had died. The book is called *Dearly,* and as you might expect, a number of the poems are about him. He was pre-mourned. Daniel Halpern—for Ecco in the U.S.—was the lead editor, Ellen Seligman having died (too young) in 2016. Becky Hardie for Chatto published it in the U.K, and Jared Bland for McClelland & Stewart in Canada.

The driving force behind the publication of *Paper Boat* has been Daniel Halpern, currently with Knopf U.S., with Becky Hardie of Chatto and Stephanie Sinclair of McClelland & Stewart (Penguin Random House Canada) backing him up. With so many different poetry publishers in my past, following the paper trail and rounding up the permissions has not been an easy task. Thank you to Robert Shapiro and also to my agent, Karolina Sutton of CAA, for helping with it. And to Heather Sangster of Strong Finish, fearless copyeditor, up to the job as always. Thanks also to the early readers of my manuscripts, a list that includes not only those already mentioned, but also Eleanor Cook; my sister, Ruth Atwood; and my daughter, Jess Atwood Gibson.

A special thanks to the many translators, from dozens of different languages, who have taken on the difficult challenge of translating my poems. Because it deals in very specific nuances, allusions, double meanings, and word flavours, poetry is the hardest form of writing to translate. I'll mention two heroic ventures: the translations into French by Christine Evain and Bruno Doucy, published by Robert Laffont; and the selected poems published as *Die Füchsin*

(The Vixen) by Berlin Verlag, with numerous translators, all of them poets themselves. These kinds of initiatives are labours of love—since they surely are not commercial ventures—and I receive them as gifts, with much gratitude.

Thank you to my readers. Without readers, no writers, and vice versa. Writing passes from hand to hand, and if you are reading this, my writing is now in your hands. To paraphrase a great aphorist, the spirit blows wherever it wishes. I hope you don't find it an ill wind.

And, as always, to Graeme Gibson, who didn't write poetry himself but was appreciative of mine, and put up with the erratic conditions under which it was written. Always a wise counsellor and constant support in times of trouble. We miss him constantly.

✦

Thank you also to those who try to keep my life in order, despite the obstacles. They include: Lucia Cino, Director of Operations at the office of O.W. Toad, who attempts to control time, and to keep mine from being all eaten up. To Ashley Dunn and Todd Doughty. Penny Kavanaugh, keeper of the books; and V.J. Bauer, tender of the website. Also Donald Bennett, Mike Stoyan, Sheldon Shoib, Bob Clark, and David Cole.

To Coleen Quinn, who takes me for walkies; to Xiaolan Zhao and Vicky Dong; to Matt Gibson; to the Shock Doctors and Terry Carman; to Randy Gardner, Evelyn Heskin, Ted Humphreys, and Junior Heath.

And finally, thanks to my parents—my mother, Margaret Killam Atwood, who read out loud to me when I was a child; and my father, Carl, a biologist who loved poetry (though nothing written much past 1920) and frequently recited poems by Walter Scott or Robbie Burns that he'd had to memorize in school, long ago.

There weren't a lot of party dresses in my young life, but there were always lots of books. That was major.

CREDITS

Two-Headed Poems. Toronto: Oxford University Press, 1978.

True Stories. Toronto: Oxford University Press, 1981.

Interlunar. Toronto: Oxford University Press, 1984.

Selected Poems II: Poems Selected & New, 1976–1986. Toronto: Oxford University Press, 1986. Copyright © 1986 by Margaret Atwood. Used by permission of Ecco, an imprint of HarperCollins Publishers LLC.

Morning in the Burned House. Toronto: McClelland & Stewart, 1995. Copyright © 1995 by Margaret Atwood. Used by permission of Ecco, an imprint of HarperCollins Publishers LLC.

The Door. Toronto: McClelland & Stewart, 2007. Copyright © 2007 by O.W. Toad Ltd. Used by permission of Ecco, an imprint of HarperCollins Publishers LLC.

Dearly. Toronto: McClelland & Stewart, 2020. Copyright © 2020 by O.W. Toad Ltd. Used by permission of Ecco, an imprint of HarperCollins Publishers LLC.

UNCOLLECTED POEMS II (1991–2023)

"Thriller Suite": First published serially in *Thriller Suite: New Poems*. Wattpad, June 23, 2012. https://www.wattpad.com/story /1563997-thriller-suite-new-poems. And as a limited edition chapbook. New Hampshire: Tungsten Press, 2018.

"The Disasters of War: A Sequel": Debuted April 22, 2024, as part of the *Beati Pacifici: The Disasters of War and the Hope for International Peace* exhibition curated by W. Bruce C. Bailey from the Bailey Collection for the Venice Biennale, running at Chiesa di San Samuele until September 29, 2024.

"My Grade Five Class Reciting 'In Flanders Fields,' Remembrance Day": Debuted May 29, 2018, as part of the Hay Festival 2018 Armistice Gala, Hay-on-Wye, Wales, and released digitally on the festival's social media.

Margaret Atwood is the author of more than fifty books of fiction, poetry, and critical essays. Her novels include *Cat's Eye, The Robber Bride, Alias Grace, The Blind Assassin,* and the MaddAddam trilogy. Her 1985 classic, *The Handmaid's Tale,* was followed in 2019 by a sequel, *The Testaments,* which was a global number one best seller and won the Booker Prize. In 2020 she published *Dearly,* her first collection of poetry in a decade.

Atwood has won numerous awards, including the Arthur C. Clarke Award for Imagination in Service to Society, the Franz Kafka Prize, the Peace Prize of the German Book Trade, the PEN USA Lifetime Achievement Award, and the Dayton Literary Peace Prize. In 2019 she was made a member of the Order of the Companions of Honour for services to literature. She has also worked as a cartoonist, illustrator, librettist, playwright, and puppeteer. She lives in Toronto, Canada.

A NOTE ON THE TYPE

The text of this book was set in Bembo, a facsimile of a typeface cut by Francesco Griffo for Aldus Manutius, the celebrated Venetian printer, in 1495. The face was named for Pietro Cardinal Bembo, the author of the small treatise entitled *De Aetna* in which it first appeared. Through the research of Stanley Morison, it is now generally acknowledged that all old-style type designs up to the time of William Caslon can be traced to the Bembo cut. The present-day version of Bembo was introduced by the Monotype Corporation of London in 1929. Sturdy, well-balanced, and finely proportioned, Bembo is a face of rare beauty and great legibility in all of its sizes.

Composed by North Market Street Graphics
Lancaster, Pennsylvania

Printed and bound by Berryville Graphics
Berryville, Virginia

Book design by Pei Loi Koay